JESSE

The true story of a dog who changed my life

Diane Barker

First published in Great Britain as a softback original in 2019

Typeset in Minion Pro

Editing, design, typesetting and publishing by UK Book Publishing

www.ukbookpublishing.com

ISBN: 978-1-913179-34-2

JESSE

b. 21/05/05 d. 25/01/17

Acknowledgements:

Thanks are due to the following:

The Barrow family who bred Jesse and let me have him

Kristina of Elmo's Kitchen for providing invaluable nutritional advice and support to us

Jonathan, the local vet, for his patience and support throughout Jesse's life

Sarah, the Oncologist who enabled us to take part in an experimental treatment programme for cancer

My friends who looked after Jesse when I couldn't be with him; especially Sue, Chris, Michael and Sheila.

Prologue: To Jesse: on the 13th anniversary of the start of our lives together

In the car, excitement mounting like the road in front of me,
I drove towards a farmer's cottage, where I knew that you would be.
All along the narrow lanes, round the corners, up the moor,
More and more impatiently towards this place I'd been before.
My purpose was to pick you up and take you home to live with me,
A new beginning for us both, beckoning us compellingly.
To be together from today, and see our lives begin to blend;
I felt so privileged to know that I would be your human friend.

You did not know that I had come to change your life forever more.
Your life with me would be so different from the life you lived before;
Good or bad, you had no choice, on that (for you) traumatic day.
Did you want to leave your home, and come with me? You had no say.
I tried to fully understand the sacrifice you had to make
By leaving everything you knew, with all your happiness at stake.
I stood and watched you as you played, wondering what I should do.
Did you want to leave or stay? Nobody consulted you.

I did the only thing I could. I swept you up and held you tight,
I felt you nestle into me and promised then to treat you right.
I looked into your trusting eyes and made to you this sacred vow,
Explaining how our lives would be forever, starting off from now.
And everything I said to you, I truly and sincerely meant.
"I'll always do the best I can to keep you happy and content,
We'll go for walks, meet other dogs, and you can play and run and chase,
We'll live life to the full together, not a moment will we waste.

I'll keep you healthy, give you treats, you'll have a happy, loving home.
Whatever happens, please believe you'll never have to be alone.
Never will I abandon you; I'll be there for you without fail;
I'll love you dearly, be your friend and laugh to watch you wag your tail.
And we'll explore the world together, have adventures by the score,
All the while becoming closer, as we love each other more.
You'll never have to feel afraid; I'll never cause you to be sad,
Our lives together will be great, I promise you, you will be glad."

Prophetic words, for so it was, such happiness I've never known
As that we gave each other, and we never had to feel alone.
Neither did I realise, when I made my vow that day,
That Jess would make his vows to me, as time went by, in his own way.
He gave me love, protection, care. He made me laugh, he was such fun,
Always was he there for me, the two of us became as one.
He gave me courage, urged me on to overcome anxiety;
His inspiration healed my wounds, brought out the very best in me.

"So thank you Jess for all your love, for all the special times we had;
You were the most amazing dog, and now I am so very glad
That thirteen years ago today I took you home to live with me.
The best thing I have ever done, and that was plain for all to see."

Contents

'A true friend is one soul in two bodies'
(Aristotle)

The incident of the seagulls: February 2006

It was a stormy winter's day. The rain was lashing against the windows and the wind screaming round the walls of the house. The sky was dark and menacing, as rain filled clouds released their burden of water without restraint.

Jesse, however, was not one for staying indoors, and the forecast indicated no reprieve. With some reluctance I put on my wet weather gear and Jesse and I headed for the beach.

When we arrived, the rain continued to hammer down, and the wind howled around us. The beach was invaded by wave after angry wave, as sea spray mingled with the rain, creating a deluge of water falling down upon us. The wind whipped the sea into a frenzy, and huge white horses rolled towards us at breathtaking speed. Seagulls, riding the currents, screamed overhead. As I battled to walk against the pressure of the wind, and my wet weather gear proved no match for the conditions, I thought, wryly, that living with a Border Collie had its drawbacks, even when the Border Collie was as lovable as Jesse.

I noted, without surprise, that the beach was quite deserted. Jesse and I were obviously the only ones crazy enough to brave this unusually harsh weather. The weather was the last thing on Jesse's mind, however. Jesse was an avid chaser of seagulls. He simply couldn't ignore them and a walk on the beach always involved his self appointed task of removing them from the beach, and returning them to the water or to the air above. He set about his work with his usual energy and enthusiasm, and I smiled as I watched them reluctantly fly off. Jesse paused for a moment to survey, with satisfaction, the empty beach, but the seagulls never stayed away for long, and soon there were more of them strutting up and down, taunting him. He was never a dog to give up easily and the chase continued.

I only started to feel a twinge of alarm when I saw him pursue them into the water, and swim speedily after them as they flew just above his head. The sea was extremely rough and there was a rip tide.

"Jesse," I called, "here!"

No reaction. I called louder and more and more urgently, but he was in a world of his own, and to my horror, followed them onto a sandbank a hundred metres from the shore. There he joyfully pursued them, barking, and waving his long tail happily in the air. He was completely oblivious to me, the weather and the conditions of the sea.

Although it was clear to me, it was not to him, that the tide was rapidly coming in. I had no idea what to do, but I did know I had to get him to come back before he was swept away or dragged under by the ferocity of the tide, when the sandbank disappeared beneath the waves.

Jesse was only 8 months old, and like most puppies, loved to play with other dogs, so I frantically looked round to see if anyone was coming, with a dog which could perhaps distract him and encourage him to swim back. But still, there was no-one in sight. I ran up and down the beach, searching for someone, and at last found a lady sheltering with her dog under the pier.

"Please help me," I said, by now desperately afraid for Jesse's safety.

"My dog is chasing seagulls onto the sandbanks and I can't get him to come back; the tide's coming in, and I don't know what to do. I'm afraid he is going to drown. Please would you come back with me and try to distract him? He loves other dogs, and if he sees yours, he just might come back to have a play."

"Oh how awful!" she said, "not on the sandbanks in this weather! However did he manage to swim out there in this? Yes, of course I'll come if it might help".

Together we ran back down the beach, but Jesse completely ignored us and her dog. Maybe the noise of the wind and rain was such that he couldn't hear us, maybe he chose not to respond. Maybe he was so absorbed in chasing the seagulls that he didn't have the capacity to take anything else in, but for whatever reason, he made no response. We stood there, helplessly, watching the tide rapidly advancing, and Jesse, quite oblivious, running round and round the sandbank, barking and enjoying chasing the seagulls which landed from time to time on the sand bank.

Eventually, I realised that I would have to go in and get him. Unfortunately that area of the beach, where the sea meets the estuary, is very rocky. I waded in, amongst the rocks, trying desperately to get to him, but the rocks were slippery and provided no secure footing, and the tide was crashing against my legs, with terrifying power. I kept losing my footing and staggering against the tide, half falling and clinging onto rocks below the waves with my hands, but it just wasn't viable, and I made no progress as I struggled with all my might to get out to the sand bank. By the time I was up to my thighs, the current was so strong that it was pulling me down and I wasn't even half way out to the sand bank. Thoughts flashed through my head of articles I had read in which people had gone into the sea to rescue their dogs and been drowned and the dogs had made it safely back to shore, and I didn't see how me drowning was going to help either me or Jesse, or my family for that matter, so with extreme reluctance I accepted I couldn't get to him, and staggered back, soaking wet, to the shore.

I was by now verging on hysterics, but I tried to keep calm and think of possible strategies to rescue him. I noted that the local trawler was just coming into harbour, so I ran alongside it, and asked whether they could rescue Jesse. It proved impossible to make myself heard, but by gestures I communicated the problem, and by gestures they communicated that they could not help. They were, quite rightly, concerned that if they went close enough to the sandbank, they would ground the trawler on it, and maybe damage it as well. They suggested I call out the lifeboat.

I looked back one last time to see what was happening to Jesse, and he was sitting still, surrounded by water. The tide had rushed in on him, the seagulls had flown away, and the sandbank had disappeared. He looked completely bemused. The small crowd, which had gathered by this time, were calling out to him and encouraging him to swim back, but he was afraid to move.

I ran faster than I thought was possible to the lifeboat station, but there was no-one there and no phone number on display.

As I ran back in despair from the empty lifeboat station, a huge cheer arose, and I came over a rise in the sand to see Jesse swimming for his life. There he was, a little puppy, battling against a tide which had defeated me entirely. I couldn't believe he could do it, but he did and I watched as he made it safely to the shore, against all the odds, as many adult dogs had drowned at that dangerous spot. He came out of the sea, shook himself and came up to me. I put him on the lead and walked him to the car, watched him jump in and only then did I believe he was safe!

I held it all together until I got home, and then in a delayed reaction, broke down in floods of tears. In amongst my overwhelming joy that he had made it, and my awe at his strength and determination, I felt frustration and anger, because by ignoring me he had created that terrifying situation, despite all the work I had put into training him to come to call.

The intensity of my feelings shocked me, as having been so afraid of losing him, I now, for the first time, fully realised how much I loved him, and how unthinkable life would be to be without him.

Jesse didn't seem to have grasped the seriousness of the situation, although he realised I was definitely not happy with him. As I dried him off, I both hugged him and berated him for his crazy behaviour and for ignoring all my patient training!

I was in such a state that I poured myself a brandy to help me to calm down!

I told him he must never frighten me like that again. He looked subdued and obviously realised that he had really upset me, but, although we had no repetition of the seagull incident, it was most certainly not the only time he gave me cause for alarm and concern for his safety. Jesse was a dog who liked to live on the edge, and at times his activities were, to me, quite hair-raising!

Eventually I felt myself again, and suddenly remembered I was due to go work. It was only mid-morning, and I hoped no-one would smell alcohol on my breath and maybe start a rumour that I had a drink problem!

The next day I took Jesse back to the beach, on a long rope, determined to train him not to chase seagulls ever again. I need not have bothered. To my surprise, he obviously had realised the seriousness of the situation he had placed himself in, it had frightened him, and he had understood that chasing them into the sea was a really, really bad idea! That day he took absolutely no notice of them! I realised than how intelligent he was, and how capable of learning from experience. People say that dogs remember, but can't reason. It may be true, but Jesse had certainly learned a very valuable lesson on that occasion, and I think it was an early indication of the high intelligence he displayed throughout his life.

It was two years before he even looked at another seagull, and although he then resumed chasing them off beaches, he never followed them far into the sea! In fact he never swam far into the sea again, under any circumstances, and never went in at all if it was rough.

However, his enthusiasm, when he did start chasing them again, was undiminished, and he did not give up lightly when they flew back onto the beach after he had chased them off. His joy was infectious, and, confident he would now chase them safely I could take great pleasure in watching him, full of admiration for his pure speed, and the beauty of the way he moved. He would bark, wag his tail, pause and then gallop after them all along the beach until they were all gone. If any returned, he was off again! Passers- by stopped to watch him, too, and admire his speed and dedication, and sometimes to laugh at his activities. Someone suggested he should be employed by the council to remove seagulls, as although they are a protected species, they are now so numerous that they cause problems in seaside areas, and can even be dangerous when trying to steal food from peoples' hands.

"Don't you get fed up with watching him chase seagulls?" asked a close friend of mine, when I told her about it.

"No, I could watch him all day", I replied, and it was true. He was so alive, and so full of joy, when absorbed in chasing seagulls, and truly in his element.

How Jesse changed my life

This is not a story about a guide dog, which enabled me to get out and about and have my independence, as so many wonderful dogs do; neither is it a story about a hearing dog which changed my life in a similar way. I am fortunate in that I have no need of either.

It is not an enthralling story of a dramatic rescue, such as me being dragged by Jesse out of a burning building whilst lying unconscious on the floor, or being saved by Jesse from an intruder or someone trying to do me serious harm, although I am sure he would have been up for either of those had the situation arisen!

Jesse was not an army dog, sniffing our IUDs and saving my life by finding one just in time, or in fact a dog with any special task to do to help a human. He was just an ordinary dog, who lived with an ordinary woman. Our lives together were certainly not without drama or incident, but this book is about the slow healing changes that occurred in my life during our time together, through shared experiences, an evolving and deepening relationship, and above all the extraordinary power of love to change and transform lives for the better. Although we were both ordinary in many ways, our relationship was not, and the result, for me anyway, was to change who I was, the way I looked at things, and the person I became during our time together, very much for the better. Our relationship also helped me to recover from a very traumatic and serious road traffic accident, both mentally and physically, and it helped him to cope with a very rare aggressive cancer which he contracted later in his life, and to make medical history by surviving for two years longer than any other dog with this condition, as far as I know, and certainly two years longer than his own prognosis, based on textbook expectations.

So this is a story about the highlights and challenges of our day to day lives together and how we stuck together, and looked out for each other, loved each other, and brought each other untold happiness.

Most dogs are notable for their faithfulness, their ability to forgive and their unquestioning acceptance of and attachment to their humans. But Jesse gave me so much more than that. In a world where so many people are critical, competitive, self centred, materialistic, and not altogether trustworthy Jesse was the complete opposite. He was brave and strong, he was fiercely protective and loyal; he was intuitive and sensitive, unfailingly compassionate and incredibly loving. At the same time, he was very much his own person, strongly individualistic, quite definite in his likes and dislikes, very determined, and had a very strong sense of fun and humour. Above all, he was so full of life. He really embraced life with tremendous enthusiasm and lived every moment to the full, and this enthusiasm was infectious. Life with Jesse was never dull or hard work; it was full of fun, exciting and very rewarding.

The irony is, that before I met Jesse, I had no intention of getting a dog, and especially not a Border Collie, as they were by no means my favourite breed of dog. It was really a series of co-incidences that led us to each other in the first place. This is how it happened.

Summer 2004

The phone rang.

"Mum, we're going on holiday to France for a couple of weeks next week, can you look after Shep for us?"

Shep was a Border Collie who belonged to my adult daughter's boyfriend.

"Um, well, I don't really know him. What about your boyfriend's mates, can't any of them do it?"

"No, we've already asked everyone else!"

"But I'll be at work during the week, and playing the organ on Sunday."

"*Please*, Mum, otherwise we'll have to put him in kennels. We're at work during the week as well, and he's used to being left."

"Well, I'd hate to think of him in kennels.........Oh, well, I suppose I will manage somehow. OK then, if you bring him down, I'll do my best to look after him."

This conversation took place nearly a year before Jesse came into my life. As I put the phone down, my heart sank. I had only met her boyfriend's dog a few times, briefly, but he had struck me as unfriendly, nervous, a bit snappy and definitely not easy to have around! In fact, to my mind, a typical sheep dog, like those I had encountered from time to time on farms which had snarled and barked and run after us as we had walked by. Also, he hardly knew me, and didn't know the house or the family (my step family) at all. He would surely feel abandoned, and scared, and I wondered however I going to manage to look after him. Also we already had a dog, a Border terrier called Polly, which belonged to my husband and I wondered how they would get on.

I was much relieved when, shortly after being dropped off, Shep settled in surprisingly well, and was soon able to relax. Not only was it not a chore to look after him, it was a joy, and we had a wonderful time together. I encouraged him to go ahead on walks and run around where he pleased, as his re-call was excellent and he was very well trained. When he realised he could go for long walks in the countryside, and on the moors, run around off the lead, and receive tons of love and affirmation, he gained in confidence, and the anxious, snappy dog I had known became a happy, loving one, whose tail was constantly wagging. I solved the work problem by taking him with me, and he was great. He was brilliant company, and I loved having him around.

When my daughter came to pick him up, she got out of her car and stopped dead in her tracks.

"Mum, what on earth have you done to this dog?" she asked. "He is so happy and relaxed. He never wags his tail like this at home. He's like a completely different dog!"

Unfortunately, although Shep had started life in the country, circumstances had changed, and he became a 'home alone' dog in the city during the week, while his owner was at work. He was also left alone quite frequently in the evenings, when they went out. It was no life for a young Border collie, and it really upset me to think of him lying there day after day with no stimulation and nothing to do except wait for the dog walker who took him out for an hour at lunch time. His owner was not unkind to him, but he was strict and Shep, being a sensitive Collie, was quite anxious around him in case he did anything wrong. The strictness of his owner had its advantages in that Shep was extremely well trained, and he was looked after well, in terms of having really good food and lots of toys to play with. His owner would play a game with him in which he hid Shep's toys round the flat and Shep had to go and find each one as his owner called out its name. This was fun for Shep, and he did well at it, rarely making a mistake, although he always looked anxious if he got it wrong. There were also good times in Shep's life at week-ends, when he would be taken out and about, and he especially enjoyed accompanying his owner on off road cycling expeditions, which gave him masses of fun and exercise.

After that fortnight when I had looked after Shep, I really looked forward to seeing him when I visited my daughter, and Shep always greeted me with great enthusiasm, but I always felt sad when it was time to say goodbye, knowing he would have those long hours on his own.

After a while I thought I had hit upon a solution and offered to have Shep during the week and return him at week-ends, to avoid putting him through the miserable life he led during weekdays, but enable his owner and my daughter to enjoy him at week-ends. It would undoubtedly have revolutionised Shep's life but they did not think this was a good idea, feeling he would have split loyalties.

Eventually my daughter suggested I might get my own collie dog, instead of getting more and more attached to Shep, so I thought about it carefully for some time.

July 2005: to have a Collie, or not to have a Collie?

Although, as I have mentioned, we already had a dog at home, she was not my dog. She had in fact belonged to my husband's first wife, who had died of cancer at a relatively young age. I don't know what sort of relationship she had with the dog, Polly, as I did not know the family when she was alive, but when I came on the scene I was struck by the fact that Polly did not appear to have bonded with anyone in the family. They did not look after her very well, and soon it was my job to feed her and walk her and generally look after her, but she never bonded with me in any way, and did not even greet me when I came home from work. On the other hand she was very friendly and would make a great fuss of complete strangers. She was not well trained, and although I made strenuous efforts to teach her to at least come to call, I never succeeded, so walks with her were not much fun, as if she was on the lead, it was dull and if she was off the lead, it was worrying because you never knew when she was going to disappear and not return for ages. My husband was also worried that she would get stuck down a badger hole, as she was a great one for disappearing down holes or trying to dig out rabbit holes. I have had dogs all my life, but never experienced anything like that, where there was no relationship and so little reward for the time and effort it took to look after her.

So if I did get a Collie, it would be in addition to Polly, and I would have to try to make sure they got on with each other, and would have to look after both.

The other factor to weigh up was that I had been badly injured in a road traffic accident six years previously, and my left leg had been crushed. It was so badly damaged that four different surgeons who looked at it and took X-rays said they couldn't save it and it would have to come off.

I have always been an active person, my main hobbies being walking in the countryside, swimming and rock and roll dancing, as well as playing music. My children had been very active, and we had spent a lot of time riding, cross country running, and swimming, as they competed in tetrathlons. Physical activity was a way of life for me, and the thought of losing a leg was intolerable. So I refused to give consent. In the end I was extremely fortunate to find a young surgeon who was willing to have a go at putting my leg back together, and against the odds he had succeeded, but it had been a long hard road, and I had been told I would never be able to walk far, and would only be able to manage on a flat surface with the help of a stick, and would have to use a wheelchair a lot of the time. I refused to accept this and worked extremely hard at recovery with the help of a chiropractor and a lot of swimming and cycling, but my walking was still restricted to about an hour, before the leg began to swell and hurt, and of course, its future was uncertain, once arthritis had set in. Would this be good enough for a Collie, surely one of the most active breeds of dog? On the other hand, would having a Collie motivate me to keep trying to walk just that little bit further and could I still make progress with my recovery after six years?

In the end, my longing to have my own dog, with which I could bond and have fun, and which I could train properly was so strong that I decided to go for it, and find myself a collie pup!

After a couple of weeks of looking, I came across an advert for some collie puppies for sale locally. They were described as mainly collie with bit of greyhound in them. Intrigued, and attracted by the idea of some cross breeding, I went to see them.

There were 9 of them, in a farmer labourer's cottage, where there were already 6 adult dogs. It was a very 'doggie' household, in which the dogs were clearly much loved and well treated. I had read, the week before, an advert for a missing dog, and it turned out that this dog was in fact the pup's mother, who had been since been found, drowned in a local reservoir. The family were extremely upset by this, and showed me loads of photos of her. She looked very much like a greyhound but with collie markings, and since they lived in an isolated area, she had been allowed to wander. Accustomed to swimming in this reservoir when the weather was hot, she had jumped in, not realising that the water level was down, due to a prolonged spell of dry weather, and then she must have found herself unable to get out again.

The pups were 8 weeks old when she drowned, which was fortunate for them as they were old enough to be weaned, and they were all strong and healthy. There were teenage girls in the family, who gave the pups loads of love and cuddles, so despite their Mum's death, they had a good start to life in many ways. I liked the look of the puppies and the whole set up seemed very genuine and loving, so I decided I need look no further and would choose one of these puppies. I spent three separate hours watching them play.

They were all so cute and beautiful! All had slightly different markings, all were black and white, except one which was almost entirely white, and all of them looked strong and healthy. Most of them looked just like collie pups, but one looked a bit more like her mother, with a definite look of greyhound about her. What fun they had! They rolled each other over, snapped at each other, chased round and round in circles, tried their luck in playing with the adult dogs (and got told off by the males!), and then flopped down, shattered, for a few moments before starting all over again. When it was feeding time, they had a large plate of food to share, and there was much shoving and jostling to get to the front and get as much to eat as possible. They were all gorgeous, and eventually I could begin to discern their individual characteristics, and where they were in the pecking order. One was already spoken for, which left 8 to choose from.

I was curious as to what Dad was like, and asked whether I could go and meet him. The farmer took me in his car to the neighbouring farm where the puppies' Dad lived.

I met him in the farm yard, where he greeted me like a long lost friend!

"Oh, isn't he beautiful!" I said to the farmer, "and so friendly. I thought working dogs were a bit suspicious of strangers?"

"Oh no, not him, he loves everybody. Anyway, he doesn't do much work these days" the farmer replied. "He spends most of his time lying around the farm yard or in the house. We had no idea that he had mated with the puppies' mother, they must have got together behind the stables when we weren't looking!"

He was a thickset type of collie, and unlike the puppies, he was long haired. His hair was very thick and wavy, he was quite small, although stocky, very friendly and extremely good looking! I decided to get the pup which looked most like him, in the hope he would turn out to be like his Dad, both in looks and temperament.

This was Jesse. He was black and white, mainly black, with a white C shape on the back of his neck, and white legs, chest and paws. He could hold his own in any of the play fights, was amongst the first to dig into the food when it arrived, and didn't seem worried by the older males when they growled or nipped at him. He was also very friendly, and loved it when I picked him up and held him close.

Although Mum had looked very much like a greyhound in height and build, she was in fact three quarters collie, only a quarter greyhound, so I hope Jesse would look just like a full collie, but with a bit of luck, be calmer in temperament, and faster because of his greyhound genes.

Having staked my claim to Jesse, I came back later with my husband to pick him up. He was 10 weeks old. I was so excited to finally have my Collie, and I was determined to give him as good a life as I possibly could. As we took him away from his brothers and sisters, and his human family, and everything he had ever known, I felt very conscious of the responsibility I had just taken on, and keenly aware of Jesse's vulnerability. The breeders had made no checks on me, or asked for any references. I could have been anybody, and Jesse had no choice...his whole life and happiness was at stake and was in my hands. I made him a silent vow that I would always do my best for him, to keep him well fed, give him lots of exercise and company, and above all, love and understanding. I was determined that he would have a happy loving home and be taken care of for the rest of his life. He deserved nothing less.

The beginning of our lives together

By the time Jesse joined us, Polly, my husband's Border terrier, was no longer with us. This was for two reasons. The first was that we had moved house, and now had a large unfenced garden, and I pointed out to my husband that he would need to fence it as Polly was an escape artist, and she would just disappear if there was no fence and probably end up getting shot by a farmer (since the house was in a small farming village) or run over. I also pointed out that I would be busy with my Collie, and whilst I would do my best for Polly, he might have to take a more active role in walking her and looking after her. Strangely, he decided that it would be too much trouble to fence the garden, and he didn't want to take responsibility for his dog, and although she had been with the family for eight years, he had little affection for her, so decided to re-home her!

I took no part in this decision, although I was very surprised to hear it, but he did a good job, and she went happily to live with a couple in a nearby town, who had a fenced garden, and wanted a dog which would be good with their grandchildren and play with them. Polly was ideal for this, as she was so friendly, and in fact she was probably happier with her new owners, than she had been with us. I did not go to visit her, but my husband did, and said the new owners had said she had shown no signs of missing any of us at all, but had settled in happily immediately!

I wasn't worried about needing a fence for Jesse, as I expected him to bond closely with me, which would be more effective than any fence in keeping him at home and safe. (Collies have a reputation for strong bonding as they were bred, as most people know, for working closely with a farmer on a 1:1 basis.)

When Jesse first joined us, I was working mainly from home. The family consisted of me, my husband and one of his two boys, the other having grown up and left home before we had moved house. The younger boy was 16. He was a lovely, gentle, open person, who was easy to have around, and quite excited by the idea of having a puppy coming to live with us.

Jesse missed his family at first, and needed lots of comforting and reassurance that he would be OK with us. Within a week or so, though, he seemed to be adjusting well to his new life. He was extremely intelligent and very quickly understood what was expected of him. Within a few days he was house trained, a process which was made easier by the fact that it was summer and so easy to be outside with him a lot, and of course by the fact that we had a large garden.

He very quickly learned what basic words meant, like 'here' and 'sit', and seemed very happy to comply. I bought him lots of toys and played with him, which he enjoyed tremendously, and training and playing became all part of the same activity. My stepson was brilliant with him, and they had wonderful play fights, growling at each other and rolling over and over on the floor.

I was the person he bonded with, however, which was exactly what I had intended and hoped for, and soon he became very much 'my dog'. Although he was very fond of my stepson, he never really took much notice of my husband, and they tolerated each other without having much of a relationship.

Unfortunately when it came to putting a lead on him, Jesse went quite berserk! He really hated it, and fought fiercely against it, leaping and plunging like a horse in a rodeo! He did everything he could to get away from it, and however gentle I was he just ran round and round pulling and tossing his head and leaping in the air in his desperate attempts to get rid of it. I decided to put that aspect of his training on hold for a while, as he couldn't go out on walks anyway until he had had his first round of injections, and eventually, with much patience and encouragement, I persuaded him to accept being attached to it. However, he made it quite clear that he accepted it with reluctance. Fortunately, as he got older, his level of obedience was such that he rarely needed to be on the lead, and in fact didn't have one for much of his life.

Even worse for Jesse was being expected to travel behind the dog guard in the back of the car. When I persuaded him to jump in the back for the first time, he scrabbled desperately against the dog guard, and howled. The sight of him jumping up at it, whilst howling in distress, was so upsetting to me that I stopped the car and removed it immediately. Although he was then still a young puppy, he was quite happy with this arrangement, and happy to remain in the back of the car, however long I left him there when I went shopping. He could easily have jumped over onto the back seats, and must have been tempted at times when I left bags of food there whilst going into another shop, but he never did.

I realised as time went on that there was a connection between his dislike of the lead, and his extreme reaction to the dog guard. Jesse couldn't bear to be confined. It was always a strong aspect of his personality, and any situation in which he felt trapped or shut in was anathema to him. Freedom was very high on his agenda. He just needed to be free, not to run off or do anything bad, just for the sake of freedom itself. By a strange co-incidence, I am claustrophobic, and I also hate being confined in any way; for example, I am quite unable to spend a day sitting in an office, or a day in the house without getting out several times for quite long periods,

I can't cope with lifts or worse, the underground or planes, so we were on the same wave length in that aspect of our personalities from the start.

Jesse was a very strong character, and had clear ideas about what and whom he liked and disliked, and throughout his life was very much an individual. He was never in any way aggressive towards people, but neither was he indiscriminately friendly. It took him a while to get to know someone, and if he decided he liked them, they would be his friend for life. If he didn't, he would just ignore them, however much they tried to win his affection.

As he grew older, I was quite surprised to see him growing into a long haired collie, as he and all his siblings had been short haired like their mother. Although this was bad news for the carpets, it was great news for me, as he developed the most beautiful fluffy coat, which always shined and look fantastic. Although I had hoped he would turn out to be very much like his father, in fact his long curly coat was probably the strongest characteristic he had inherited. He was quite a lot taller, a much stronger personality, and despite my theory about the greyhound genes making him more 'laid back' he was in fact really quite neurotic at times, and quite crazy in the way he hurled himself around, chasing balls or other dogs or birds or animals!! No-one could ever have described Jesse as being 'laid back'!

Training Continues

When Jesse was around 6 months old, he decided that, although he understood what I wanted him to do, he didn't necessarily want to do it. He knew how he was expected to behave. However, rather than conform to expectations, he was much more interested in having fun, and in his eyes, fun usually meant chasing things. Bicycles, tractors, cars, scooters, skateboards, roller skates, runners, in fact anything that moved, was fair game for Jesse.

Then there was the whole world of nature surrounding him with animals and birds to chase. As well as seagulls, he loved to chase pheasants, and would also run miles following finches, as they flew just above his head, in flocks, dipping close to the ground and then flying up out of his reach again. However, most irresistible of all, to him, were deer. Fortunately, he didn't often come across them, but when he did, he was gone, silently and at tremendous speed. I very rarely saw the deer, or him going after it. He would simply disappear, and then I would hear excited barking in the distance. The only solution was to await his return, when he was usually covered in mud, and panting in exhaustion.

Like many puppies he would make for any smelly substance he could find on walks and take great pleasure in rolling in it.

As we were walking along a narrow country lane one day, I heard a distant rumbling sound. That meant a lorry was on the way. This was unusual, as the lanes where we lived were so narrow that they were rarely used by lorries. I had not come across one before whilst walking Jesse and wondered how we would manage. When this one appeared it was a milk lorry. They were the worst, the biggest of the lot! I squeezed Jesse into the hedge and pressed myself in front of him in the hope that the lorry could get by. The driver summed up the situation and was not happy.

"Pick the collie up", he shouted, through the open window. In horror I looked down at Jesse, who had just excelled himself in the art of rolling and was covered in badger droppings, surely the smelliest of all. I hesitated, squeezed us both in more tightly and looked appealingly at the lorry driver. But it was no good. His mind was mind up.

"Pick him up!" he shouted more loudly, thinking I hadn't heard him. I had no choice but to hold Jesse tightly, as close to me as possible, as the lorry inched by, but it was not a pleasant experience!!In fact, it was quite disgusting and we both went straight into the bath as soon as we got home!

Jesse soon learned not to roll in smelly substances, not because I told him off, but because he was clever enough to work out that rolling in muck always resulted in being hosed down or put in the bath, and he did NOT enjoy baths and even less being hosed down! He continued to roll throughout his life, but very soon confined his rolling to clean bits of grass or sand.

He was also determined to eat various animal droppings and ignored my attempts to dissuade him. In order not to spend walks shouting at him, and since our area was very rural and it was impossible to avoid animal droppings , I tried giving him a biscuit if he dropped what he was eating when I told him to. Jesse was enthusiastic about this, but it backfired on me. He soon actively sought out animal droppings, especially horse manure, and would bring it proudly to me, wagging his tail and looking up expectantly, so he could have another biscuit. It was impossible not to laugh! Typical of Jesse, that he didn't in fact totally defy me, he did drop the stuff he picked up, but he also tried to do his own thing and have the best of both worlds! The issue resolved itself as he grew older and lost interest in this particular activity. However, another problem soon reared its head.

"Diane, can't you stop that dog digging up my garden!" came an anguished cry from my husband.

"Look what he's done, just look at it! This is a beautiful shrub, and he's destroyed it. *You'll* have to stop him, he takes no notice of me at all!"

He was quite right. Jesse loved digging. I don't think he intended to uproot shrubs and flowers; they just got in his way. My husband was tearing his hair out as yet another shrub was upended and Jesse appeared with soil all round his mouth and a happily wagging tail.

It was not easy to resolve this, as Jesse was on his own in the garden at times, and it was confusing for him, as he was allowed to dig as much as he wanted on the beach, where we spent a lot of time walking. One day I had a brainwave! I thought he might like a sand pit, where he could dig happily without upsetting anyone, and claim as his space. My long suffering husband was persuaded of the value of this idea, and created a lovely large sandy area where Jesse could dig without spoiling the garden. Unfortunately, being Jesse, he decided he didn't like it, and took very little interest in it. Eventually, as a result of my patient but persistent training, he understood that digging was OK on the beach, but not in the garden and the problem was resolved.

I spent a lot of time training Jesse, and put a lot of effort into it. My theory was that hard work and time spent training Jesse at this stage would be rewarded by many years of peaceful co-existence when the training was complete, and although training Jesse was frustrating at times, and needed patience and understanding, it could also be very rewarding.

I realised the only way with him was to get him to WANT to do what I asked, and the only way to do that was to build a strong relationship based on love and trust. When I called him, I held out my arms, caught him as he rushed up to me, and hugged him. I tried to make training a game, where he was always set up to succeed, and then made a huge fuss of him when he did. Training sessions were short, and followed by games with a ball or a soft toy. I found that if I waited until Jesse did something of his own accord, like lying down, sitting or coming towards me, I would respond with the relevant word, as he did it, so he soon began to associate the two.

Given Jesse's enthusiasm for action, and his boundless energy, it was not, perhaps, surprising that he pulled hard when I walked him on the lead. He resented the lead, anyway, which he regarded as a quite unnecessary restriction, and was most unwilling to walk along by my side when on the lead.

My training to get him to do this without pulling was unconventional, but very successful. For ten minutes a day for a week, I walked him alongside a wall, by my left heel. In front of him was a plastic bag filled with cotton wool balls. If he tried to pull, his nose would bump into the bag, which he didn't like, and also he couldn't see much in front of him to make him to go ahead, so he just walked alongside me. I added the word 'heel' every so often, and after that week, he never pulled on the lead again. He had also learned what 'heel' meant, which enabled him to walk to heel off the lead as well.

Domestic dogs interestingly have more in common genetically with wolves than they do with wild dogs, which are still to be found living in packs in Africa, amongst other places. It is said that our domestic pets have 99% the same DNA as wolves, although some breeds (e.g. Malibous) have a stronger genetic resemblance than others (e.g. toy poodles).Wolves have a clear hierarchy from the Alpha male and female downwards, which is accepted by all, although challenged on occasion when there will be fights to establish supremacy. Therefore it strikes me that dogs are more comfortable with living in a hierarchical structure where they are clear as to where they stand. If their human friend does not take on the role of the Alpha male or female, there are some dogs who get frightened and confused and feel unsafe, and others who will happily step into that role themselves. The problem between me and Jesse was who was to be the Alpha male /female? We both wanted this role and I embarked on some techniques to stake my claim to it! When I put his food down for him, I told him to sit and wait a few seconds before eating it, and I never allowed him on the furniture, because I felt it was important that I was seen by him to be literally 'higher', and have some places which were just for me and other humans, as part of our 'top dog' status.

One day, as I put his food down, I realised I had forgotten to add something to it, and went to pick it up again. To my amazement, he growled at me, warning me off, so I just took it anyway, knowing he wouldn't hurt me, and also that this was important, and a very good opportunity to emphasise my 'top dog' status. I put it out of his reach and went out of the room for a couple of minutes, much to his consternation! I then returned and put it back down, making him wait a couple of seconds for permission to eat. This had the desired effect as he realised it was not acceptable for him to try to tell me what to do. He never growled at me again if I had cause to pick his food up before he had finished.

For the sake of safety, I made him wait for permission to jump out of the car, however keen he was to go on his walk, and he was never allowed to cross a road until I told him to go.

It didn't take long to establish my authority and he accepted it gracefully and after that, training became incredibly quick and easy. Once Jesse had decided he wanted to please me and do things I asked him to, he learned very quickly, since he was so highly intelligent. I never had to ask him more than twice to do a new thing, and he would understand what I meant and just do it without any fuss, or me having to repeat myself. Everything hinged on our relationship and the love and trust which was growing all the time. Jesse proved at different times of his life that basically he only did what he wanted to do, and he was such a strong personality that it would have been a very foolish thing to try to force him to do something through harshness or rough handling. He would have just fought back. The key to Jesse's heart was love, respect and feeling secure, and I felt privileged when he handed me that key.

As Jesse progressed through his life he became exceptionally well behaved, in that he just did whatever I asked him to do. It was at this point that I didn't bother taking a lead with me, as he really had no need of it. He would walk to heel, sit quietly under the table in a pub or cafe, come as soon as I called him, cause no trouble with other dogs, wait to cross roads...the list went on. But then it occurred to me that it is possible to have a dog which is actually too well behaved to fit society's expectations!! This was when I noticed signs, which I had not previously been fully aware of, which said: 'Dogs must be on leads'. These signs appear quite frequently in cafes, pubs, shops, and on public footpaths where there may be livestock in the fields. This was tricky when you didn't have a lead! We had two amusing incidents in which Jesse and I got caught out by these signs, and after that I always tried to remember to put a lead in my pocket, much as it would annoy Jesse, to please the general need of our society to feel reassured that dogs are under control (perhaps with good reason in many cases)!

The first occasion was when we went to a furniture shop. They had an item in there which I really wanted to see, as I had seen it on their website and thought it was exactly what I needed. However, when I went in with Jesse walking to heel, the assistant said that dogs were only allowed on the lead. I didn't want to leave Jesse outside because the shop was on a main road and I was worried about traffic fumes (although I knew he would stay put and wait for me), and anyway I think it's illegal to have a dog on a main road without a lead; and I couldn't leave him in the car since we had come by bus. So I explained how well behaved Jesse was, but I could see the assistant had reservations. I asked him if he could spare us a minute and said he could (fortunately the shop was empty except for us). So Jesse and I did a quick display for him. We walked round the furniture, every so often stopping still, with him stationary by my side; then I asked him to sit, stay, come, go round the back of me, sit again, lie down, and resume the close heel walk, weaving in and out of the furniture on display. After a couple of minutes I asked:

"Are you happy now for him to come in off the lead?"

And he agreed he was! He had been most impressed and asked about training schools and advanced obedience courses. But I told him it was just Jesse and I, and how we'd evolved this way of being together which worked really well in these types of situations!

The second situation was trickier. We had just come across a beach which was new to us in one of our exploration expeditions. It was low tide and there were vast stretches of golden sands with no-one much around. It was very beautiful, and we had a wonderful time. Noticing there were paths off the beach onto a type of uncultivated land, I thought it would be interesting to explore this as well, and was glad that we had, as there were lots of wild flowers and areas of grasses and lakes and beautiful reeds swaying in the wind, as well as lots of birds and insects flying around. Jesse was walking next to me, when we came across a man in uniform who turned out to be a Park Ranger. Apparently this was a nature reserve, but having come in at the end of it via the beach, I hadn't realised.

"Please put your dog on the lead," He said, firmly.

"I'm terribly sorry, but I can't because he doesn't have a lead", I replied.

"Well, he can't come in here without one" he declared, in a very assertive manner.

This struck me as slightly bizarre, because the fact was he was already there. Racking my brains for an acceptable solution, I suggested we might retreat to the beach by the nearest exit. But he wasn't happy with that, as it would mean Jesse going through some of the reserve off the lead en route. So I asked if there was a quicker exit we could take, to get out of this very awkward situation, but was told there wasn't. I had nothing I could substitute, such as a belt or a piece of string or handbag strap, so we were a bit stuck. I asked him whether he had anything he could lend me as a substitute lead, but he replied in the negative. Eventually, after we had stood there in silence for a while, I promised him faithfully that Jesse would not disturb the wildlife, and promised that he would walk to heel throughout as we left the area as soon as possible. Otherwise, as I pointed out, we would be stuck there forever and still Jesse would be contravening rules by being off the lead. I added that I could quite understand the need for the rule, but our presence there was just by chance as we were strangers to the area, and I would ensure, on any future, occasion that Jesse would be on the lead. Privately I was thinking how ridiculous the whole situation was, as Jesse was clearly under control and had been from the beginning, and given the fact that I didn't have a lead for him, and his attitude to being on the lead, I was hardly likely to return anyway!

Eventually the Ranger relented and allowed us to leave the area by the quickest route, but although I fully applauded what they were doing, and fully understood that dogs chasing wildlife was totally inappropriate in that setting, I couldn't help feeling he was being a little rigid in his approach on that occasion!

Jesse and sheep

Walking through a field which had a public footpath across it, I was amazed to see Jesse note that two sheep were grazing alone, and the rest were in a pack together. He weighed up the situation, and slowly trotted over to one of them. Gently he encouraged it to move towards the flock, and he guided it at a walk and then a trot until it was safely re-united. He then went to the second sheep and repeated the procedure. This was a dog who loved chasing things and had had no training whatsoever in herding sheep! What an amazingly strong instinct he must have had, and how strong his genetic heritage must have been.

Before taking Jesse into a field in which there were sheep, I had realised that it was very important to train him not to chase them, as a collie which chases sheep has a real chance of being shot by a farmer. Knowing his love of chasing things, I had been really concerned to ensure that he fully understood that chasing sheep was not on the agenda. The question was, how could I do this safely? I decided to approach a local farmer, and ask whether I could go in her fields to train him with her sheep.

"I'd rather you didn't" she said!

Perhaps I should have explained myself better, as she might have thought I meant train him to round them up, rather than train him to leave them alone! She suggested I should look out for a field with a public footpath through it and sheep in it, so I could take him in legitimately and train him there. It was not long before we found a field that fitted the bill, which was why we were in this field in the first place. On the first occasion, I put Jesse on a lead (despite his objections) and ventured on through the field. He took a great interest in them but made no attempt to chase them. Then I returned with him on a long rope, and all went well. It was on the third occasion, when he was off the lead, that he gently herded the two sheep back to the flock. I could hardly believe my eyes, when I saw him do this, and was not only very impressed, but relieved, as I realised I would never have a problem with Jesse and sheep. And I never did. He always treated them with gentleness and respect, and left them alone unless he felt the need to get them all together!

By the time he was a year old, I had a fantastic, loving, fun, yet obedient dog, whom I could take anywhere, knowing he would behave appropriately and safely.

It can't be easy to be a dog in a human dominated world, where so many of their instincts are regarded by us as unacceptable, and they have to learn to behave in ways which don't come naturally, and in some cases, are quite contrary to their instincts. And yet they do it, if properly trained with love and clarity. I wonder how easy we would find it to fit into the world of a wild dog pack; probably extremely difficult, although there have been occasional stories of babies brought up by wolves who have survived and adapted.

After his first year, Jesse didn't need a lead any more, except on a main road, for legal reasons, and since I never took him on main roads because of the noise and the pollution, he didn't actually have a lead for most of his life.

Because Jesse was so good and loyal, I was never had to tie him up if I went into a shop which wouldn't take dogs. He just waited outside, and I was completely confident that he would stay there and would never have dreamed of going off with a stranger, or just wandering off if something caught his attention.

Walks with Jesse were fun and relaxing and interesting. There was no stress, because I knew he would not do anything wrong and would return if he went off anywhere to investigate something. I rarely needed to call him, and if I did, I knew he would come.

However, it was a different matter with my husband. Although perfectly amicable with him at home, Jesse never did anything my husband asked him to, totally ignoring him. It was the same with well meaning friends who told him to sit or called him on walks. He completely ignored them. He really was a one woman dog from the start!

Love between Jesse and me

I sometimes wonder what this story would have been like if Jesse had been able to write it himself, from his point of view. I don't know how different it might have been, but one thing I do know for sure, and that is that this is a story, not only about our lives together, but also about love.

Love was the key word to describe my relationship with Jesse. I loved him from the moment I picked him up from the farmer's cottage where he was born, and every day I loved him more, however impossible this might seem. How I loved him, and how he loved me. We were part of each other, rarely apart, and almost telepathic. He completely changed my life and taught me what love is really about, and how it feels to be truly loved by someone loyal, unchanging and totally accepting. He made it possible for me to love him with my whole heart, without any reservation or fear of rejection, and to experience the joy of loving so completely.

I have photo of me, dozing in the sun on the lawn, with Jesse, at 12 weeks, sitting right over me, almost on top of me, already guarding me and watching over me. It speaks volumes.

It was this love and closeness that paradoxically gave us both more of the freedom we valued so highly. Because of Jesse's faithful and unchanging love for me, with no reservations or conditions, I began to gain in confidence, and my self-image, always rather fragile, improved.

This was a hugely important thing for me, as I had had a difficult childhood which had resulted in me growing up very lacking in confidence and having very poor self esteem. This was so deeply rooted that it marred my life to a considerable degree, preventing me from meeting people, stopping me from doing so many things out for fear of failure, and worst of all, leading me into difficult relationships with unsuitable men, which only confirmed my sense of worthlessness. My relationship with Jesse slowly but surely began to change all that. I began to feel more confident, and less restricted by fear of failure. Jesse had confidence in me, and I could feel him supporting me with his love and trust, and telling me, in his own non-verbal way that if I did fail, he would still love me and be there with me just the same.

It is a strange paradox, I feel, that, as humans, we find it difficult to accept people exactly as they are. We have this urge to just alter them a bit, mould them perhaps into being what we would like them to be, to fit our own needs rather than theirs, especially within a close relationship. The effect of this, on me anyway, is to make me lose confidence, and become neither completely myself, nor the person they seem to want me to be. When someone loves you unconditionally, you can accept and love yourself for who you are, and become fully your best self, hence frequently becoming a better person. Jesse was the only one in my life who ever accepted me entirely as I was, and as a result I felt a slowly growing confidence which applied to my life at work, my musical activities, and my social interactions with people. It also affected our walks and exploring new places together. In that area of our lives he enabled me to enjoy going to isolated but beautiful places, not knowing quite where we would end up, or what might happen, but confident that with Jesse, we would be able to have a new experience safely and enjoy it together. I knew if anyone approached me aggressively Jesse would have defended me with his life, so when I was with him, I never felt afraid, wherever we were. I also stopped worrying about getting lost. My sense of direction is not the greatest, but Jesse's was, and there were many occasions on which Jesse confidently led us in the right direction back to where we needed to be.

I gave him the confidence to be the dog he was designed to be, and to be loved and appreciated for it. He needed me to understand him and fully appreciate his need for freedom, and to have confidence in him and give him the trust he so richly deserved. He was such an individual, with such strong likes and dislikes, and so full of life and enthusiasm. Although he respected me and my wishes, it was because of the love between us, and his early training. I did not try to control him through anger or fear, but if I needed to ask him to do something it was through love, and this enabled him to be fully himself. A different type of relationship between us might have destroyed his confidence and increased his tendency to be neurotic. He could have been quite a 'difficult dog', because of his strong personality, and his need to do his own thing, but in fact, by loving and understanding him, I freed him up to become just the opposite, a remarkable and exceptionally happy and confident dog. I also helped to free him from some of the negative consequences of his rather neurotic personality, as I could calm his fears, and encourage him to overcome his anxieties, by patience and giving him the confidence to turn to me for reassurance, which he knew he would always receive. In this way, I could also feel so much better about myself, because I knew I was wanted and needed when I gave Jesse the support he needed and could see him responding positively to it.

Our love for each other, in my experience a rare privilege, was to prove the key to so many things in our lives; the way he helped me to overcome mobility problems following the car accident; the way he helped me to cope with the psychological difficulties it had created for me, and especially, in the end, the way we managed his final horrible illnesses.

By the end of those difficult 6 months, when he was coming up to his first birthday, he had complete trust in me, and I in him. When we went for walks I very rarely called him or asked him to do anything; he was just there with me, and if he went anywhere, I knew he would come back. If there was a noise, like a motor bike backfiring, or thunder, Jesse would be frightened, but I would do my best to reassure him, and eventually would manage to convince him it would be OK. Whenever there were fireworks, he was scared, so I tried to ensure that we were never outside when fireworks were being set off, but safely inside. I made sure I was there with him; I would never have left him alone if there was a chance of fireworks being set off, or a storm in the offing, and he found that as long as he could hide under my legs, or lie next to my bed, if it was late, I could stoke him, and comfort him, and he could manage. He did not want a 'special place' in the house to make him feel safe, as so many dog books and websites suggest, he wanted me, and my reassurance. He fully believed that if I told him he would be OK, then he would be OK.

At home, he always insisted on sleeping by the front door, so he could guard the house, so that was where I put his bed. He took this duty very seriously, although it was a self appointed one, and I never felt afraid, during the times I lived on my own with Jesse. Although he was in no way snappy or negative towards people, he was very clear in his mind about who was OK and who was not, and his bark could be very ferocious, although he never, ever, attacked anyone. However, I suspect that if anyone was thinking of breaking into the house, Jesse's bark would have put them off, and if they had persisted, he would probably have gone for them.

I have had quite a few dogs in my life, starting with a Corgi when I was 10 years old. They have all been fantastic in their own different ways, and all loving, obedient, fun and loyal. I have loved them all and given them the best life I was able.

But Jesse was completely different from the others. He wasn't just my dog, he really was my best friend and my soul mate.

The Common

When Jesse was still quite a young puppy, and while his training was still a work in progress, we had several adventures which made me realise just how important it was to him to chase things. This was one of them.

It was a lovely mellow autumn evening, and dusk was approaching after a beautiful sunny day. We were walking on the local common, a Site of Special Scientific Interest, and a very popular place with many people, including me and Jesse. Many different varieties of heather were in flower, with their range of shades of purple, and the gorse, smelling strongly of coconut, glowed golden amongst the heathers. The leaves of some of the trees were just beginning to turn. Apart from the singing of birds, there was a peaceful silence. My husband accompanied Jesse and me on this walk and we were breathing in the beauty and tranquillity that surrounded us. Inhabitants of the common included flocks of tiny chattering birds, which would swoop high and then low down to the ground, some kind of finch, I think. Jesse was fascinated. He had seen them before, but never really taken them in, perhaps because there was so much else to see and smell, and perhaps because they were swooping very low over us that evening, and there were lots of them. Some of them stopped to perch in the trees, but most kept up this pattern of flying, high and then low. He watched them for some time, started to slowly wag his tail, jumped up and down on the spot for a bit and then took off in a flash, galloping beneath them at full speed ,trying to keep up. Over and through the gorse and heather he ran, up and down the hills, through the trees, and no sign at all that he heard our increasingly frantic calls to him. We could hear his excited barking receding into the distance as gradually the light began to fade.

Still waiting for him, some half an hour later, wondering whether to split up and search for him, or whether one of us should search and the other stay put so Jesse would know where we were, we heard someone coming, and it was with great relief that we saw, emerging from the darkness, a lady leading a very tired, bedraggled Collie puppy, which she said she had encountered at the other end of the large expanse of common. It was Jesse, of course! Fortunately she had caught and rescued him, found us, and enabled us to take him home safely.

However, despite this unfortunate incident, we continued to walk on the common, although not at dusk until Jesse was better trained!

There were lots of areas of scrub, and large tracks cut in the scrub as fire breaks. These were perfect for walking, as were the many little tracks that led off in different directions, through grass and trees, copses and brambles. At one end was a pine forest, and at the top there was an awesome view across miles of farmland to the moors, about 15 miles away.

Jesse and I loved this special place, and spent a lot of time, especially in his first three years of life, going for walks there. We would go looking for blackberries together in autumn. I would eat the ones at the top of the bush (and pick a few) and Jesse would eat the ones at the bottom. He was enthusiastic about this initially, but when he got older he lost interest and left me to it! We also collected sticks for kindling for the wood burning stove. Jesse was great at finding sticks, but less keen on handing them over;

nevertheless, we enjoyed doing it, and managed to take a few home. We had a real sense of being together on walks which I valued very highly.

So many walks, so many lovely times together that they almost all merge into one, but there were a few times which stand out in my mind, as unusual things happened.

It was very early in the morning, and as we walked on the common we came across one of the travellers, who had a semi-permanent encampment there, walking five large dogs. We were some distance away, but we could see them quite clearly, and Jesse began to make his way towards them. The traveller saw us, and shouted to his dogs, which did not respond. He then began to run at top speed towards them, trying to get hold of them before they saw us. I realised that they were probably unfriendly and kept as guard dogs, and called Jesse to me immediately. He came back straight away, and we stopped and awaited events. The traveller managed to get to all five of his dogs, catch them, and get them under control and back behind the fenced camp where they lived, before they saw us and made a move towards us. With a sigh of relief, Jesse and I moved on, and finished our walk. I suppose he walked them so early to avoid meeting people with other dogs, and was alarmed and surprised to see us, and when I fully realised what could have happened- a pack of large guard dogs attacking one small puppy- I was quite horrified. From then on, we avoided their area of the Common, and we never saw them again, but I was grateful for his quick thinking and responsible action in getting them all out of harm's way so swiftly.

The second occasion was quite amusing. Jesse was a bit older, and we were both pretty familiar with the Common by then. Sometimes we would see the local farmer, who also ran a livery stable for horses, out for a ride, and cantering along with a few others on one of the wide spaces. Jesse often looked at them, but never tried to join them. On this occasion, however, he changed his mind, and the temptation to gallop alongside them proved too strong for him. He rushed over to join them, with his tail waving happily in the air, and ran alongside them with much enthusiasm, but not barking or jumping up at them.

"Will you stop your dog annoying my horses?" she shouted to me.

By this time I had lived in the village long enough to get to know her a little and we got on quite well, and had a similar off beat sense of humour.

"I will, but only if you stop your horses getting in the way of my dog!" I shouted back.

Laughing loudly she increased her speed and they continued on their way, but I did call Jesse and he returned to me immediately. I didn't want to spoil his fun but there were safety issues for him, and the horses and riders, and she was right to object to him joining them, however well-intentioned he might have been!

The third occasion took place on a lovely hot summer's day when we were wandering around, enjoying the weather and the beauty of the natural environment. Suddenly an adder slithered across the path in front of us. Jesse stopped dead, his hackles rising, and seemed uncertain as to what to do. I was also taken aback, as I had never seen one before, although I knew they lived on the common, as they featured on a large board which showed species to look out for. It also warned people to avoid them, as they could attack if they felt threatened. I knew they could attack dogs, and in fact I had heard stories of them actually killing dogs. So I thought it best if we both just stood still, Jesse and I, and waited as it slithered across the path and disappeared into the undergrowth. I think all three of us were taken by surprise and wanted the same thing...to get away from each other with no harm done to any of us! It was a beautiful creature, however, and lovely to have a chance to see it close up. We never saw one again, although a lot of people I met on the Common said they had seen them, and there were also stories of attacks by the snakes on dogs, which probably barked at them and caused them to feel under threat.

Deer

Walking in the local area, through some woods, I suddenly realised that Jesse was no longer with me. He was still young, about 9 months, but I had come to expect him to accompany me on walks off the lead without any issues.

"Jesse! Come on" I shouted in the encouraging way I had developed with him, but he did not come back. There was no response.

"Jeeeee-sssseee" louder. No sign of him.

I called and called getting increasingly frantic. Where was he? Why had he disappeared and why hadn't he come back? Was he caught up in some brambles or undergrowth? Had he somehow wandered off and got disoriented?

All these awful thoughts raced through my mind, and I soon I just stood there in complete silence as there was no-one else around and no sound, even of bird song. Walking up and down, searching the area, without having any indication at all of where he was, I wondered whether I was doing the right thing. What if he had returned to the place where he had disappeared, and found I wasn't there? What would he do then? Should I go back, or should I keep searching? My anxiety levels went through the roof. I called him from time to time, but there was no sound at all and still no sign of him. Maybe he was a long way out of earshot by now and couldn't hear me anyway. I felt completely helpless.

It was the most horrible feeling, and no solution seemed to present itself. An hour passed, and eventually I went home, which was just up the road, and had a cup of coffee to try to calm down. I then returned, to the place where I had last seen him, still unsure of what I could do. My heart missed several beats! There he was, sitting in the place where he had left me, looking a bit guilty, very muddy, with thorns sticking out all over him, but undeniably pleased with himself and happy. I was so delighted to be re-united with him, I could hardly believe it was him, just sitting there, safe, and back with me at last.

Sadly this was not to be a one off occasion, and I soon realised what had taken him off like that. He had seen or smelled a deer.

All his life, he was fascinated by deer and absolutely loved running after them or with them if possible. He would see them, deep in the woods, long before I did, and disappear silently before I realised he had gone. I didn't know there were deer in the area where we lived, as they are very shy and will conceal themselves whenever possible, and in fact even when I knew they were living in the woods around the area, I still very rarely saw them. Jesse's attraction to them came as something of a shock, especially when he disappeared out of sight so quickly, and would often not re-appear for some time. When he finally did, he was usually covered in mud, panting in exhaustion, but very happy. I was not, however. It is incredibly worrying, if you love your dog, to hear him in the distance, in thick woodland, crashing around and barking, and then to be confronted by an ominous silence and no sign of him at all. I would stand there, worried sick, wondering if he was OK, or maybe caught up in a thicket, or lost, or hurt, since he crashed around with no regard at all for where he was going or his safety, and I also was worried that he might not be able to find his way back.

Unfortunately there were several places near us where deer lived, and it wasn't possible to walk him locally in places where I could be sure there would not be deer. I would have to hatch a plan to modify this behaviour.

Before I had had a chance to do this, I foolishly took him for a walk in a forest nearby, with many hectares of coniferous trees and walkways between them. I should have realised there was a likelihood of deer living there, but sadly did not until too late. We were about half an hour's drive from home. Jesse did his disappearing trick. We were neither of us familiar with the area. I called him until I was hoarse, and walked miles trying to find him, or hear him crashing around or barking, but only heard silence. I was at a complete loss as to what to do as one hour went by and another started. At this point I met a man with an Alsatian on the lead. I told him of my dilemma, and he told me that his dog had done the same thing, only he had not found him all day. Eventually he had gone home after dark and returned the next day, but to no avail. Later on the second day, someone else had come across him and returned him safely. I was absolutely horrified, and couldn't imagine going through such an experience with Jesse. Fortunately about 10 minutes after this conversation, I met Jesse trotting up the path, looking lost and very guilty. I don't think I had ever been so delighted and relieved to see him. We never went there again for a walk; it just simply wasn't worth the anxiety.

However, something had to be done to stop this disappearing which was beginning to create real anxiety for me and spoil our walks together.

"You should just keep him on the lead, so he can't run off," said a number of well-meaning dog walkers, as they observed me peering anxiously into the distance, and calling fruitlessly when Jesse was on a deer chasing expedition.

"But how will he ever learn to come back, if he isn't free to go in the first place?" I inquired.

"You can't keep a Border collie on the lead for ever, they are bred to run free, and they need to be able to do this".

Anyway, I thought to myself, keeping Jesse on the lead he hated so much was not a possibility. He loved his freedom, and it would have completely broken his spirit to have walked him on a lead.

It is a tricky issue in dog training, to my mind, the issue of teaching a dog to come to call at times when he is strongly tempted to follow his own instincts and wishes. If he doesn't come back for ages, and then you are cross with him when he finally reappears, even though this is an understandable reaction, it will not work, as he will associate returning with being told off, and may even become scared of coming back if you are really cross. On the other hand, if you make a fuss of him when he comes back after a long period of ignoring your calls, he will naturally assume that it's OK, and he is doing the right thing. It took me some time to get to grips with this issue with Jesse, as he was so passionate about doing his own thing, unlike some dogs which are happy enough to trot along beside you, and have no wish to go far away from you.

In the end I decided that I would try to be vigilant, and look out for deer, and call him as soon as he saw one, in the hope of preventing him from going off in the first place. If I failed to do this, I would call him very strongly and loudly, and if he came back within 10 minutes, I would make a big fuss of him, and demonstrate how pleased I was to see him, but if he kept me waiting for more than half an hour, I would silently put him on the lead and terminate the walk, either by going straight home or returning to the car. I would then ignore him for a short period when we got home, say about 15 minutes, and then resume my normal behaviour towards him. He soon caught onto this, and his long absences became fewer and eventually ceased altogether. Whether this would work with a less intelligent dog is hard to say. It would have been impossible to keep up with him on his deer chasing expeditions, so I don't know exactly what went on, but I suspect that the 10 minute period covered him chasing a deer, losing track of it and returning. The longer period must have involved him chasing a deer, losing it, and then searching for more. So I presume in his mind, the compromise was that he would return when he lost the deer, rather than regard the chase as the beginning of a deer hunt. I was very rarely quick enough to see the deer and call him straight away, but if I did, he would not chase it but just come to call.

In the meantime I continued to walk him off the lead every day in interesting places which we both enjoyed. We were fortunate to have the choice of many lovely walks close to where we lived, and one of them I always thought of as the 'pheasant woods'.

These were peaceful, deserted woods, full of beautiful trees, especially in autumn, with their glorious range of colours, and were inhabited by numerous animals and birds, because so few people ever went there. For me it was a fantastic place to spend an hour exploring, walking and just breathing in the atmosphere. The wood had a main track through it, and a few side tracks, leading off into the slopes and bushes along the sides. Every walk could be slightly different from the last.

Jesse loved these woods as much as I did, but for a different reason, as he enjoyed the wonders of nature in a rather different way! Walks in these woods followed a similar pattern every time we went. As I would walk through, enjoying the atmosphere and letting my thoughts wander, Jesse would vanish into the undergrowth. Then there would be a sudden disturbance involving a rustling in the bushes and deep within them I might glimpse the white tip of a black tail!

A loud alarm call would rend the air, and a pheasant, in its gloriously coloured plumage, would fly off, indignantly and clumsily, to the tree tops. A few seconds later, Jesse would appear, in hot pursuit, tail and nose in the air, following the path the pheasant had taken until he could see it no longer. He was always sorry to see them go, and I'm sure he wished he could fly! But since he couldn't, he would accept defeat reluctantly, and start all over again, and once more I would hear the odd rustle in the bushes, and then the above scenario would be repeated. Jesse loved it, and I loved seeing him so happy. Of course we couldn't go there in the breeding season, but at all other times of the year, we could, and I don't think any trained gun dog could have bettered his flushing out technique. He never caught a pheasant, but I don't think he wanted to particularly. I think he just enjoyed the excitement of the chase!

For a few short weeks of the year, we would have access to stubble fields, after harvest and before ploughing. We often walked through some of these which were local and afforded a fantastic view of the sea. Jesse would be sniffing around, often not far away, and suddenly, a partridge would fly up, almost from under my feet! Again he would follow until it disappeared from view and then set to work to find another. It is amazing how well camouflaged these birds are, and how still they can be. They could fool me any day, but not Jesse!

When we walked on the marshes, he would look speculatively at ducks which would be swimming in the dykes, and then suddenly he was off, chasing them through the water and way across the marsh, hurling himself after them wherever they went, until they flew off, quacking loudly. Even then he would follow them until they were just specks on the horizon. Geese, however, he wisely left alone!

The great thing about Jesse chasing these birds was that they could easily and quickly fly off, which meant they were unharmed, and I didn't often lose sight of him! It also meant that walks were never dull. Jesse lived life to the full, and his enthusiasm was infectious. It never worried him that he couldn't catch the birds he was chasing. They just gave him the opportunity to enjoy running and test out his speed against that of other creatures. To him it was an exciting game which he never became tired of. To me, it was a spectator sport which I enjoyed and added some spice to a walk. Whatever the weather, or the location, a walk with Jesse was always, for both of us, fun, unpredictable, a pleasure and a joy.

In the meantime, Jesse was getting to be a mature dog, and our walks were getting longer and more adventurous. At first I hardly noticed, but then I realised that my left leg had stopped protesting after an hour's walk, or if I walked uphill or over rough ground. It was fine! No longer was I confined to an hour's gentle walking. With Jesse that hour became an hour and a half, then two, and I was climbing banks and going over rough ground and exploring new places, and my left leg was just fine. Not only was it OK for well over an hour, but it could go again later that day as our walks became two full length ones rather than one long one and a play with the ball in the park for the other one. I had become so caught up with Jesse's enthusiasm and with watching him rush around and enjoy himself that I simply hadn't realised what was happening to me, but when I did, I was overjoyed. The healing capacity of the body never ceases to amaze me, and I am over awed by it. After 6 years, my leg was still improving, still strengthening, and just by walking, as I had stopped cycling and swimming after I had Jesse, and no longer needed to see the Chiropractor.

The moors and other walks

At weekends Jesse and I would sometimes go up to the moors for a walk. We both loved doing this, especially enjoying the sense of space, peace and closeness to nature which is so much a part of being on the moors, in all but the most popular tourist areas. One of the places I love the most is a valley with a river running along the bottom, typical of the moors in that the water bubbles over a shallow river bed, punctuated by rocks, which you can treat as stepping stones, or, when you find a larger one, you can just sit on and relax, dangling your feet in the water, enjoying the feeling of being part of the river. Alternating with these shallow areas are pools of deep water, where you can swim if you can brave the cold, or just enjoy watching the pure, clear water where you can see right to the bottom of the river and spot brown trout. On a sunny day, I used to love watching the patterns of the sun on the ripples of the water, watching dragon flies and other water creatures. After a while, the path by the river comes to an end, and then you have a very steep climb amongst some small ancient trees to get to the top of the moor, where the view is spectacular, and you can return via the moor. Jesse loved this walk too. He would splash around in the river, join me on the stepping stones and nose about while I sat and watched the water and the wildlife in it.

We were about half way through this walk one day, and had just got to the top of the steep hill, when Jesse took a great interest in a gorse bush.

It turned out that a doe and her faun were lying in the bush, in the hope of escaping notice. I had never seen deer on the moor before, so it did not occur to me that it could be a deer, and I was just wondering what he was so interested in when she jumped quickly to her feet and shot off away from us with the faun following. They were so close to me I could have reached out and touched them, but her only interest was in getting away from danger, and danger meant Jesse. Ironically he would never have hurt her, but when she started running, so did he! Unfortunately she chose to go down the steep hill we had just climbed, and Jesse was gone before I had a chance to realise what was happening and call him back. Within seconds they were out of sight, and probably of earshot too, since there was no sign of Jesse returning when I called him. I was worried about all of them, especially the faun, so I climbed back down the hill as quickly as I could, and followed the path back the way we had come. He had long since stopped barking, so I had no idea where he was. Rounding a bend, I suddenly came across him, standing nose to nose with the faun, both wagging their tails. I stood and watched them silently for a while. There was no suggestion of aggression; Jesse didn't chase deer to catch and hurt them, he just loved running with them. Although I looked out for her anxiously, I saw no sign of the mother, and I very much hoped she was nearby, as Jesse and I walked back to the car.

This was a walk we did quite frequently, and I reflected on how amazing it was that I should be climbing over stepping stones, up and down steep hills, over rocks, walking and climbing for a couple of hours at least and having no pain or dysfunction. Sometimes I tried to imagine the Physiotherapist's face if she could see me now! She was the last of several Physiotherapists to whom I was allocated following the car accident, and I was unable to do the exercises she gave me due to the levels of pain they caused me. Her response was to threaten me that I would never walk again if I didn't do them, so I stopped seeing her, and worked on my recovery in a way I could manage. It would have been good to see her now though, and I suspected she would never have believed me if I told her how far and how easily I could now walk, climb and enjoy arduous and strenuous activity with no pain, rather than languishing in a wheelchair, depressed beyond belief! I would not have believed it myself at the time, and without Jesse I am quite sure it would never have happened.

That was the only time we met a deer on the moor, fortunately. If there were no birds to chase, Jesse would just enjoy the wide open spaces and being able to run as much and as far as he wanted.

On another occasion, whilst walking on the moor with Jesse and a friend, we decided that it would be fun to climb an outcrop of rocks. Some of these rocks are quite easy to climb and on a clear day you can see for miles around, once you have reached the top, and fully appreciate the unique beauty of the moorland landscape. It never crossed my mind that Jesse would have a problem, as he was always up for everything, and happily scrambled across rocks on beaches, and jumped groins, styles, five barred gates and anything else which got in his way on a walk. Jesse, however, regarded the rocks with great suspicion. Strangely enough, he came to one of his irrevocable decisions, which was that he was not a climber, and had no intention of becoming one! He hated being left behind, when I started climbing, but despite a lot of encouragement from me he was just not up for it. He became very upset and ran round and round them, but he would not set one paw on any of them! I think he was scared, although he would never have admitted it! It was no great sacrifice for me not to climb the outcrop of rocks, so after a few failed attempts to get him to join me, I decided to give the rocks a miss and just enjoy walking with him and seeing him happy that we were reunited.

Skateboards

Jesse started life wanting to chase everything that moved, not to harm it, but because he loved galloping along at top speed, and to have something to spur him on was a challenge he found hard to resist. It was all part of his enthusiasm for life, and the interest he took in everything around him. He just wanted to join in! It was easy to persuade him not to chase cars and tractors. He soon realised cars were too fast and he quickly lost them and therefore lost interest in chasing them. Tractors, on the other hand were too slow to be any fun, and anyway he didn't like the noise and rattling they made. People on bikes, horses cantering and runners were more interesting to Jesse, as they were accessible and went at around the right speed. However, when he realised I really didn't want him to chase them, he stopped doing it, although I'm not sure he fully realised why I was opposed to it.

Skateboards and scooters posed more of a dilemma for me, though, because Jesse was very keen to chase them and I had to stop him on the grounds of safety. It was difficult to train him to leave them alone, firstly because we rarely saw them-there weren't any in our village- and secondly because when we did, they were usually to be found in a skate park, and although Jesse looked at them longingly, it was easier to stop him going into the skate park, and let him know it was forbidden territory, than to deal with them whizzing past him individually.

However, on one occasion we were taken by surprise and Jesse's urge to chase the skateboard proved impossible for him to resist.

We were walking along a path which was designed for pedestrians and cyclists, and Jesse was running along ahead of me as usual. He disappeared round a corner in the path. Suddenly I heard anguished shouting on the path ahead, but since I couldn't see what was going on, I hurried round the corner to find out.

"Get 'im off me!" a teenage boy was screaming , when I came into view.

"This dog's vicious, it shouldn't be allowed, it knocked me off my board and tried to bite me".

He was holding his skateboard in front of him like a shield, and Jesse was looking up at it longingly. He had unexpectedly come across this boy skateboarding along the narrow flat footpath, (not designed for skateboarders) and he had been unable to resist the urge to run after him.

"Well, I'm really sorry he jumped up at you and frightened you, he's only a young dog and he gets over excited sometimes. I didn't realise you were there until I came round the corner and by then it was too late to stop him. I certainly wasn't expecting to find anyone skateboarding along here. I don't think he attacked you, though, or tried to bite you, he is not vicious in any way, and he likes teenage boys."

"I'm going to report you, it's dangerous, it did go for me, and bit my arm and my leg." This was said in an intimidating, aggressive manner.

He was not obviously going to be appeased easily. He certainly looked shaken, but in all truth, although it must have been frightening for him, he probably knew, as I did, that he shouldn't have been there in the first place, as the path was definitely not intended for skateboarding.

I was quite certain that what he said was not true. Jesse had never shown any signs of wanting to bite anybody, and it would have been completely out of character for him to have done such a thing.

“Oh dear, that sounds very serious” I said.

“Please can you show me the marks his teeth have left, then?”

I spoke politely and calmly, trying to avoid escalating an unpleasant confrontation.

Of course, there were none, as Jesse had just become over excited, and jumped up at him. He loved teenage boys, and was quite used to them, since he lived with my stepson, and played with him and his mates frequently. Again I apologised for Jesse’s behaviour and the fact he had given him a scare, but nothing was bruised but the boy’s ego, as he probably felt he was not living up to his ‘cool’ image by being so shaken by a dog jumping up at him.

He went on his way, muttering to himself and Jesse found himself on the dreaded lead, and the subject of much disapproval from me. He learnt from this however, and he never tried to chase anyone on a skateboard again, or jump up at them.

Scooters

As we were walking along the crowded promenade in the local sea side town, having just had a walk on the beach, Jesse spotted, (before I did) a young child on a scooter. This was unexpected as most children use the purpose built scooter park nearby. He gave chase, although he knew he was not supposed to. I immediately called him back.

"Jesse, NO!".

"Jesse, COME HERE!"

Although I called him loudly and clearly, there was no reaction. The child was frightened by this big dog running alongside him, and scooted faster and faster in the unrealistic hope that he would outpace Jesse. I became increasingly alarmed, because I knew the promenade ran out onto a road, where the traffic was heavy and the child was heading ever faster towards that spot. There was no sign of any parents, although the child was quite young.

"JESSE COME HERE THIS MINUTE!" I bawled, in a very angry voice at full volume, not knowing what else to do, as I had no chance of catching them. I very rarely called him in this way, as it was quite contrary to my principles of training him through encouragement and praise, not threatening and fear, but it was a potentially dangerous situation, which could have had very serious consequences.

My heart gave several thumps as he hesitated, and I repeated my command in a similar manner. He stopped, turned back and trotted towards me with great reluctance and a very guilty expression on his face. The child stopped, and was safe. I made a fuss of Jesse and told him to sit and stay by me, and felt quite weak with relief.

A woman, standing nearby had witnessed this event from start to finish. She turned on me and said how disgusting it was to treat a dog that way, shouting like that, and I gave all dog owners a bad name. *She* would never shout at *her* dog like that. I already felt very upset and shaken by the situation, and I could have done without her interfering and unhelpful comments. I felt so annoyed, in fact that I responded in a way I would not normally do. I made an instant decision that, if, having witnessed the event, she couldn't see the danger the child was in and the dilemma this posed for me, there was no point in me trying to explain it to her. So I thought I would get my own back, and inquired where her dog was, since there was no sign of it. She told me they had put him in kennels when they came down on holiday (as I had suspected).

"Sounds a great way to treat your dog," I said, nastily." I guess he's having a fantastic time shut up in a kennel all day. He's lucky to have such caring owners. I'm sure he's having much more fun than he would have been if he had been sharing your holiday, joining you on the beach and enjoying exciting walks in a new area!"

She walked off in disgust, but Jesse had learned his lesson and did not chase scooters again!

As for me, I was learning to stand up for myself, through standing up for Jesse! This was a great improvement on my previous rather negative self view, where I would have assumed that any criticism was justified and taken it as deserved and let it feed into my low self-esteem. I was gradually beginning to see that I was not always in the wrong, and that other people could be unpleasant and critical without good cause, and feel the confidence to do something about it. Even when Jesse was being disobedient he was helping me overcome some of my demons!

Jesse and music

I am a church organist, pianist and singer, and music has always been an important part of my life.

I was fortunate in that when Jesse came into my life I was playing in a rural church, where I knew the Vicar well and he was happy to welcome Jesse into the church whenever I wanted to bring him in with me. So it was that when Jesse was 3 months old, he found himself inside a church, listening to me practice the organ. Church organs vary greatly, but they usually have two manuals (keyboards), one above the other, and a row of foot pedals on the floor, which you play with your feet to provide the bass notes. It was not long before I felt confident that Jesse would behave well enough for me to be able to take him with me to the church choir practice, and shortly afterwards he made his debut at his first church service. Perhaps for the first time, he noticed my feet playing the pedals, or maybe he had been silently watching, without me realising, while we were in the church when I was practising, but for whatever reason, he chose that day to take action!

"Whatever was that strange noise on the pedals?" asked the Vicar, laughing, after the service. "I've heard some weird harmonies, but those were really weird!"

I had not been playing the organ long, and learning to play the foot pedals is probably the most difficult thing about it. However on this occasion it was not me who had made a hash of playing them. Jesse had been watching my feet with fascination, and had succumbed to the urge to join in. I was concentrating so much I had not noticed him eying up the pedals and watching closely, until suddenly my feet encountered his paws, and an appalling noise ensued! In a total panic, I couldn't think what to do, but then I gently eased him off while continuing to play as best I could on the manuals! I think Jesse gave himself a bit of a shock when he walked across the pedals. I don't think he had previously made the connection between treading on them and the deep resonant bass notes this created, and I'm not sure he entirely liked the noise or volume of them. In any event, he jumped off very readily, and viewed the pedals with some suspicion after this, never trying them out again! The look of shock and initial disbelief on the Vicar's face when I told him it was Jesse playing the pedals was quite funny, and general laughter followed, as the news that Jesse had taken up playing the organ spread round the congregation!

I am not a natural performer, as I get very nervous, and had been reluctant to start playing the organ in the first place, but organists are hard to find, and the one at our church had simply become too old to play anymore, as her fingers were curled up through rheumatoid arthritis. I was playing the piano in the church's music group at the time, which I found less intimidating, as I was playing with others, but then I was asked whether I could transfer my skills to the organ. With reluctance and the help of a brilliant teacher I did so, but it was always a source of anxiety for me. After that first unfortunate service which Jesse attended, his presence did in fact give me confidence in a strange sort of way. I felt that even if I made a mess of playing and maybe people were cringing or criticising me, Jesse would always love me and support me. Simply through his loyalty and total acceptance of me, he gave me the courage to go on trying to improve and accepting that sometimes I would get it wrong, and it wasn't the end of the world!

Fortunately for me, Jesse loved music. Whether it was because he was brought up with it, or whether he would have loved it anyway, I don't know.

Whenever I played the piano at home, Jesse would silently arrive from wherever he had been in the house, and lie under the piano, where he would stay until I had stopped playing, and the only conclusion I could reach is that he enjoyed the sound of the music, and wanted to listen. This, of course, encouraged me to play more, as music practice can be hard work and a bit solitary, but with Jesse there, it felt like something we could share.

He always came with me to choir practice, and became an integral part of any choir I was running throughout his life. He also took an active role in running the choir. If they went flat, he would softly but distinctly start howling! If they continued to go flat he would howl a little more loudly, but he never howled when they were in tune! All the choirs I ran found this funny, but it was also helpful to me, as I didn't need to keep nagging them, and they learned more easily to recognise flat notes and sing more often in tune.

"We must have gone flat again!" someone would say, when the howl began to compete with the music in volume, and other choir members would stop singing and start laughing.

"I'm afraid so!" I would answer, and we would run through the piece of music again until Jesse was satisfied.

After a few years of playing the organ, I became proficient enough to obtain a better job at a much bigger church. There were lots of different types of services there and a permanent four part choir.

When I went for the interview, I was much daunted to see the church, a huge Victorian building on a main road, with a large church hall attached. It was a far cry from the little village church at which I had been playing, and I was terrified! In fact, I very nearly turned straight round and went home, giving the interview a miss, as I felt convinced I could never be good enough to meet their expectations. And then I thought about Jesse, and how he was so brave and up for everything, and how if he wanted something he would just go for it. He never let a dyke or hedge or gate get in his way if he was chasing things, and if he lost sight of a pheasant he was chasing, for example, he would go and look for another. He never rolled over and gave in if a dog attacked him. Jesse would have just had a go at the interview and if it hadn't worked, he'd have tried again at another church! So I took a leaf out of his book, screwed up all my courage, went for the interview and, to my amazement, got the job!

Despite the fact that the church already had a choir, the church wardens were very keen to start up a Gospel Choir.

"Do you know anything about Gospel music?" they asked me, shortly after I had been appointed.

"We really want to start up a Gospel Choir, and there are lots of people we know who are keen to sing with us, if we start one."

"No," I said, "absolutely nothing". Their faces dropped.

"That's what the last organist said".

"But I can find out," I said. Again, I amazed myself. Who was I to start a choir in a genre of music which was completely unknown to me, and was mainly sung by people of colour, with their fantastic musical sense and ways of moving which can be difficult to emulate for more reserved white people, which we were? This was yet another example of Jesse's influence on me, and his belief in me which had gradually boosted my confidence during our time together, almost without me realising it.

So that is what I did! I listened to Gospel music on Youtube, and began to understand the off the beat rhythm and close harmonies which are so characteristic of this genre of music. I learned about its roots in Spirituals, and listened to different choirs and found the best...London Community Gospel Choir and even more so the Soweto Gospel choir, world famous and at the top of its game. I came to understand the way in which it is sung, and appreciate the fact that it is rarely written down, but learned by ear and involves a lot of improvisation. Finally I discovered that the nearest gospel Choir was about 20 miles from us.

I phoned them.

"Hello, my name's Diane Barker and I would like to start a Gospel Choir at our church. The problem is, I know very little about it and have never sung Gospel music before. Can you help me?"

"Yes, of course, that's great news. Why don't you and anyone else who is interested come along to some of our practices and join in? That's the best way to learn, just follow the others and get a sense of how it works. You would be welcome any time."

"Thank you, we'll do that. It's really kind of you."

He was very kind and welcoming and invited us to attend their next practice.

"OK, we'll see you next week then, and thanks a lot".

I reported the results of my investigations back to the church wardens and they were delighted. So it was that the following week, six of us (and Jesse) climbed into a people carrier belonging to one of the church wardens and went to join the practice. We got there more or less without incident, ably assisted by his new Sat nav, of which he was very proud. The choir met in a village hall. There were about 20 of them. The man in charge greeted us warmly and turned to the choir.

"Hey guys, we have some people from ****with us tonight. They have come to learn about gospel music, so please make them welcome and let them sing along with us".

He suggested we mingle with their choir members, joining whichever section we felt was right for us. The practice started. What an experience! They sang one song after another, all three sections singing their different parts, only using written words and no written music, and we just joined in as best we could. It was not just getting the right notes, but adjusting to the different way of singing that Gospel involves. First of all, people singing in Gospel never stand still. They always move in time with the music. Not individual dancing, but just swaying in time, together. This is not as easy as it sounds, as you all have to move at the same time and in the right direction, to avoid collisions and spoiling the whole choreography of the piece! Also in Gospel music there is a lot of clapping to emphasise the rhythm, which is an important part of each song. But the clapping has to be done exactly together and in time, on the second beat of the bar otherwise it just sounds a mess. So there were plenty of opportunities to get things wrong! No-one seemed to mind!

I have spent time in Africa and in Papua New Guinea, and heard indigenous people singing in this way; it sounds great, but the difference is that they were born and raised with this kind of music, and it comes naturally to them and the sound just flows from them, and we most certainly are not!

It was really enjoyable, though, and we had a wonderful evening. They made us so welcome and the whole experience was exhausting but exhilarating. On the way home we couldn't stop talking about it, until we realised, that is, that we were not, in fact, on the way home. The Sat nav was not doing the business, it was dark, and all it said was 'turn left'. We went round and round in circles, ending up in tiny country lanes, no-one having any idea where we were, craning our necks in the dark to try to read the occasional sign post which we passed, but instead of getting worried we just laughed and laughed. The whole evening had put us in such a good frame of mind-there is something very uplifting about Gospel music- and we had this wonderful sense that we had started something exciting, a new project, which would be a really positive venture. Eventually someone recognised where we were, and we arrived home, tired but very excited.

We attended about 8 practices and then their choir leader came and did an all day workshop with us in February 2009, to help us launch our own Gospel choir.

It was quite amazing how fast it grew. Soon we had a professional jazz pianist, who gave her services for free, and a drummer who was brilliant. We also acquired a female and male soloist, both of whom were fantastic. Our numbers grew, as many people, religious or not, enjoy this kind of music. We got our heads round the rhythms, the harmonies, and the movements, and became a fully fledged successful choir. In our first year, I wrote to people and organisations, offering to bring the choir to sing for free at their event, but by the second year, they were writing or phoning me and asking us to come. We had 30 members (I would not let it go above that, as I felt it was important for choir members to know each other, and gel as a group) and a waiting list.

We had lots of gigs arranged in lots of different places, very rarely in churches, and it was great fun and took up a lot of my time. I found myself conducting the choir in venues such music festivals, choral concerts (for which people paid to get in) holiday camps, and even the annual performance for charity at the local theatre. Jesse was always there, enjoying it, being well behaved, so I knew he would stay with me even at outdoor venues, and he was regarded as the choir mascot. It was truly a very special time in both our lives, and I could never have done it without Jesse. Never would I have had the confidence to even imagine I could be capable of running such a large and popular choir, and all the arrangements it took, and the people I had to negotiate with.

Throughout Jesse's life, I went on to play at several different churches, and started 3 more choirs. I played and the choirs sang in lots of different venues, and I very much enjoyed my musical life. Jesse was always there, always supporting me, always behaving well, always loved by choir members, and he gave me a great deal of confidence. As I said earlier, I am not by nature a performer, being too lacking in confidence, and it was only after Jesse died, and I found I was unable to play or sing for quite a long period, that I fully appreciated the confidence he had given me by his unquestioning loyalty and support, and the fact that he had enabled me to lead musical activities which I would have previously considered quite out my league.

Jesse always enjoyed choir practices, and would greet each member of the choir as they came in before settling down to listen.

Although a lot of choir practices took place in churches or church halls, one choir practised in the local pub and this was Jesse's favourite venue. He was not a dog to make friends with people quickly, and was generally quite reserved, but in this instance, Jesse and the landlord hit it off with remarkable speed. This could have been because it did not take Jesse long to realise that the landlord was also the chef!

At the beginning of choir practice, while people were gathering and chatting, Jesse would position himself just outside the kitchen, (he would have considered it quite wrong to go into the kitchen itself) and wait expectantly for the landlord to appear. He would then simply look up at the landlord, with his appealing expressive brown eyes, and before long pieces of sausage, roast meat and even steak would come his way! Much as he appreciated this, he would always rejoin the choir as soon as practice started, being a very loyal dog who knew what his priorities should be!

He also had an intuitive sense of what was appropriate, and when he came to performances, he never made a sound, even if the choir went flat, and never wandered off or caused any kind of disturbance. He just knew the difference between practice and performance.

"I didn't know there was a dog in the church" people would often say after a service, a performance, a wedding or a funeral.

"Where was he? He didn't make a sound. How did you train him to be so quiet and still for such a long time?"

The usual response was forthcoming from me.

"I didn't, he just understands what to do."

He was frequently invited to church weddings for which I was playing the organ, and would never disturb the proceedings, but watch with interest. I often thought that if, by some terrible mischance, Jesse and I lost each other, away from our home area, he would probably make his way to the nearest church. He spent so much time in churches that he probably regarded them as a second home!

Jesse at work

I was fortunate in having a job which involved visiting organisations all round the county, and was able to take Jesse with me. He received a warm welcome from the people I went to see, and was always well behaved at work. I was able to take him for walks between appointments, and he adjusted well to this way of life. Although he would run and play with enthusiasm on walks, as soon as a meeting began, or I was having a discussion with someone, or just observing what was going on, he would lie down quietly until I was ready to go, knowing that after the meeting there would be another chance to let off steam. I never had to tell him to lie down and keep still; he just thought that this was the right way to behave.

One hot day, I was late for a meeting.

"So sorry I'm late," I said.

"Not to worry," said the manager, "can I get you a drink?"

"Oh, yes, please. A pint of cold water would be fantastic!"

This was duly given to me and I put it on the floor beside my chair. When I got round to picking it up, it was quite empty, although upright. Jesse grinned up at me. I hadn't realised dogs could drink out of a glass, without upsetting it! He was quite right, of course. I should have remembered to ask for a drink for him as well!

The grin was one of many endearing things about Jesse. He had a definite grin, and when he smiled and wagged his tail, not only I, but also many other people found him quite irresistible.

I don't know why Jesse always behaved so well at work, as I had never trained him to lie by my chair and be quiet, he just had a sense of what was expected, and never seemed to need me to take notice of him, or to need to get up and wander around the room or annoy people, or make a noise. It made working life very straightforward, and most importantly, meant I didn't have to leave him alone at home. I met many people in the organisations I visited who also had dogs and said they could never have brought them into work, as they would have been too disruptive, and how did I do it with Jesse? I was unable to enlighten them.

My job was to run seminars for managers and assistant managers of care facilities, mainly in the children and young people sector, and ensure that the information disseminated was put into practice. My students were obliged by the Government to obtain relevant qualifications, and it was my job to guide them through, and in the end make a judgement about whether or not their knowledge and work was up to standard. I was the only person in the county's Workforce and Development Team to be doing this job, so had no -one for support and exchange of ideas. Sometimes it would seem quite daunting, as shortcomings in managers tend to lead to a poor service for vulnerable people, so it was very important that I helped them to get things right. On the other hand, I did not want to been seen as someone judgmental and intimidating, as apart from anything else, it is hard to get a true picture of what is going on if people are nervous or feel the need to cover things up and be less than honest. It was a very responsible job, and quite intimidating for me as well as my students! In many ways, having Jesse with me helped. He was a distraction for people, who enjoyed seeing him, and especially for the young people in the Care Homes who enjoyed playing with him, and as many of my students were dog owners or dog lovers themselves, it gave us something neutral to chat about, whilst I was trying to put them at ease. I think it also made me seem more approachable and more like 'one of them' rather than a formal distant person from County Hall.

At one work place, where I spent a great deal of time, there was a fantastic walk within 2 minutes drive. It consisted of many hectares of agricultural land and copses with a public footpath right across it. Lots of the fields were sloping, but at the top, there were extensive views and a wonderful flat field which was full of wild flowers in the summer. There were poppies, cornflowers, big daisies, and many other varieties of wild flower which I am not able to name. We were so fortunate to be able to visit this walk frequently and the wild flower meadow was a wonderful added bonus for me, especially since they are now, sadly, so rare. In the summer there were cows or sometimes bullocks, and Jesse was suspicious of them at first, and reluctant to go past them. For once he was not tempted to chase them.....he knew his limitations, and in a group they could look quite intimidating! However, I would just march through them confidently saying, saying:

"Come on Jesse, just stick with me" and he would stick like glue to my side and slink past. They were used to people and never troubled us in any way, so eventually he got used to them and just ignored them as they did us.

Border Collies as pets or working dogs?

"That's cruel that is, keeping that collie as a pet, when he was bred to work and be outside all day, working with the farmer and the sheep, using his brain, running around and living an outdoor life. He wasn't ever supposed to live in a house and be a pet."

Strangely, during the first couple of years of Jesse's life, I was told this by a number of people. Looking at the farm dogs in the village, which spent most of their time shut up in a barn, barking, it struck me as an odd thing to say. The local sheep didn't need moving every day, and if the dogs were lucky, they got a ride on the quad bike once a day, when the farmer went on his rounds checking the livestock. They may have had a chance to run round a couple of fields en route, and maybe some proper sheep dog work once or twice a week, but it didn't strike me as the most exciting life in the world! I think it is a romantic illusion that working collies spend their lives rounding up sheep in the great outdoors, with the exception of those who live in Wales or Scotland, or perhaps on the moors, where uphill sheep farming is the norm. Too many spend their lives tied up, in barns, fed on scraps and given little thanks for their efforts when they do their best to do their job well. For a loyal, loving and fun dog like Jesse, it would have been a horrible life, and I am glad he was a 'pet', my pet anyway!

I wrote earlier about training Jesse not to chase sheep and in so doing discovered that he seemed to have a natural genetic ability to move them gently and appropriately without frightening them.

Having spoken to several farmers and small holders who have sheep, I have discovered to my surprise that this is quite unusual. Apparently it is difficult to find a good sheep dog, and if you do, they are worth thousands of pounds! Common problems are being too aggressive, and nipping the heels of the sheep when rounding them up, or even ignoring their training and actually attacking the sheep. This is because the work of rounding up sheep is based on the collie's natural instinct to chase them, and the training has to channel this instinct into something more constructive and helpful to the farmer. Other problems are that some dogs are too timid and therefore intimidated if a ram stamps its foot, and so unable to do the job; some are unable to work at a distance from the farmer, although function well when the farmer is nearby; and in some cases, the dogs are simply not interested.

Jesse would undoubtedly have been an excellent working dog, as he had courage, was able form a strong bond with a human, was very willing to do as asked, extremely bright at understanding what was expected, and neither timid nor aggressive. Even so, I had no regrets! The farming community's loss was my gain, and we were both very happy together, so he didn't appear to be missing out on anything.

Another thing people insisted was that he needed to do Agility classes to keep his brain active. I am not a great 'group' person, and had no wish to do this, although I would have done so for Jesse's sake, if I had felt he needed the stimulation. Also, I am not competitive, but I was told the local Agility classes were. Although Jesse would have enjoyed running around and negotiating obstacles, he always loved to play with other dogs, and I thought he was likely to have caused havoc, putting the other dogs off their tasks, and been continually told off for socialising, which in my view was not a great idea. Although I was repeatedly told that he needed more stimulation than just being a pet, we seemed to be OK as we were and forged a life style that suited us both. My work provided us with a constant change of scene and different walks, we played with toys and balls and sticks and were really quite happy just to be together, we really didn't need anything else.

Jesse, the beach and other dogs

"That dog", said a very old man who used to sit regularly on a bench on the promenade, "that dog, loves the beach!" And how right he was! The beach had everything to offer Jesse; other dogs to play with, lots of space to run around, a less muddy alternative in winter to the countryside (Jesse never liked mud, avoiding it at all times unless he was chasing something), sea to swim in when he got too hot, seagulls to chase, games with the ball, stick chasing in the water...doggie paradise!

When Jesse first came to live with us, I took him regularly to the beach nearby in order to socialise him with other dogs. It was pretty much guaranteed that at low tide, the beach would be full of dogs of all shapes and sizes and temperaments. Jesse was a typical puppy in that he was fascinated by other dogs, and just went boldly up to them and tried to initiate a game. He would rush up and down the beach, which was a long one at low tide, playing with any dog which was willing. Often he would completely disappear from sight, and I would continue walking, confident that he would still be on the beach somewhere, and eventually we would run into each other, both equally relieved to be re-united! Sometimes he wasn't successful in his efforts to persuade other dogs to play, and he began to learn which dogs to approach and which to avoid. He began to have particular friends which he would look out for. His closest friend, when he was around a year old, was a female Alsatian. When the Alsatian's owner and I ran into each other, the dogs would race up and down the beach delighting in each other's company. It was a sad day when they moved to France, and we saw them no more, but he had several other friends, mainly bitches!

Otherwise, walks on the beach continued to be enjoyed by both Jesse and I. At first Jesse was reluctant to swim, but when I went in swimming, he didn't want to be left behind, so he would follow me and swim around with me. We spent many a happy hour on the beach. As well as a place for walking and playing, it was also a place where conversations took place between dog owners, and views were exchanged, problems discussed and advice given.

When Jesse was about 2 years old, I had some very useful advice from an elderly man with a collie, whom I met on the beach. The problem was food. Jesse went through a phase of not wanting to eat. I tried him with all sorts of different dog foods and he was just not very interested. I didn't want him to end up eating scraps or human food, as I wasn't sure what to give him, and was concerned that it could lack essential nutrients, so I became increasing worried, as he became increasingly thin. He remained active and appeared happy and healthy, but I felt we needed to sort this out.

When I saw this gentleman on the beach, his collie was really quite fat, so clearly didn't have the same problem as Jesse. I approached him and explained what was going on. He was very helpful, and told me he had had similar problems with his dog, but had found adding liver and mackerel to his dog's diet had worked wonders.

" Liver and mackerel", he declared, firmly, "that'll sort him out!" And so it did. Just a little, added to his usual food was enough to encourage him to start eating again with enthusiasm.

After he was neutered, Jesse's attitude to food changed completely, and he became very keen to eat as much as possible, and was no longer fussy about what he ate, although he was never one to scavenge on walks.

Back on the beach, Jesse was particularly keen on a game we invented, which we called 'wallie ballie'. This involved me throwing his ball against the wall which went up from the beach to the promenade. The stone slabs on the wall were uneven, so the ball would ricochet off in all sorts of strange directions, and Jesse would have to work out where it was going and catch it. He really loved this game and became very good at it. It enabled him to use his brain, as he sometimes found just chasing a ball a bit tedious after a while.

Frequently in the summer, when the town was full of visitors and we played this game, we would attract a crowd of onlookers who would cheer him on.

"Hey, mate, come and look at this dog! He's really good at catching a ball"

"Where is he?"

"Just down there on the beach, look at that!"

Faces would appear over the edge of the promenade, and peer down at us playing our game. They would be joined by more and more, as family and friends were summoned, and onlookers wondered what was going on.

"How did you train him to do that?"

"I didn't, he just loves to do it," I would shout back, as Jesse hurled himself in all directions to catch a wayward ball, or waited for it to come down after a bounce off the wall sent it flying upwards, and then leapt up high to intercept it.

"He has very quick reactions".

"He should be on the tele!"

Applause was not uncommon, and often people counted the number of times he caught a ball before missing one. When he got too hot, Jesse would trot down to the sea and swim in a dignified circle in order to cool down. Eventually the people would drift away, in search of other entertainment, but Jesse never got tired of this game, and in fact refused to pass the spot where we played it unless I got the ball out and he could spend some time playing his game!

Although we both loved being on the beach, we discovered it had its dangers. A lot of people throw pebbles into the sea, sometimes for fun, sometimes for their dogs to chase. I disagree with this on the grounds of safety, so do not take part. Jesse, however, was fascinated, and always rushed up to people who were doing this and hurled himself into the water to try to retrieve them. I always called him away, and removed him to another part of the beach if necessary.

One day the inevitable happened. I was not quick enough to stop Jesse chasing some pebbles into the sea, and he ran after them for a few minutes before I caught up with him and stopped him. I thought no more about it until the following day when after some straining he passed four quite large pebbles through his system. Amazed that he had been quick enough to catch them (most dogs just look bemused when the pebbles sink to the bottom of the sea), but relieved that he had managed to get rid of them, I felt vindicated in my feeling that the practice of throwing stones for dogs was not only dangerous but potentially harmful to their health.

Later on that day, Jesse seemed uncomfortable and kept stretching out his front legs. I took him straight to the vet's. The vet took one look at him and arranged an emergency operation. A large pebble had got stuck in his intestine and was blocking it. This would have killed him had it gone unnoticed and not been removed. Thank goodness for the vet's correct diagnosis and instant treatment. Never again was Jesse allowed to go anywhere near people throwing stones!

The Island in the River and people in hats

Collies are not generally known for their love of water, but Jesse was an exception, and although he didn't swim a long way, he loved swimming in rivers as well as the sea, chasing sticks into the water and retrieving them, and just generally splashing around. Every walk in the summer had to include water of some kind, as he had a very thick coat and rushed around so much he need to cool off on a regular basis.

There was a walk we went on quite frequently; lovely meadows, with a public footpath through them. They were bordered by a shallow river, which included an island in the middle of the river at a point about half way through the walk. In order to access it, you had to clamber down a steep bank, and in the summer, it was then just a question of walking over some shingle and then out to the island, which had some quite deep fast running water on the other side. Jesse used to climb down the bank, and go over to the island, waiting impatiently for me to join him, and then we would begin the search for suitable sticks. Once they were found, I would throw the sticks in the water for him to retrieve, and we would play for ages which we both really enjoyed. He refused to walk past the island, even in winter, insisting on this routine, so I always had to go down the river bank and in winter, wade through quite deep fast running water to get to the island, and search for suitable sticks to throw, until at last he would get tired of fetching them. He didn't appear to feel the cold, even on really frosty winter days. It was just part of that particular walk and part of Jesse's routine, and being a dog who liked routine, he was determined to do it! Unfortunately he often didn't retrieve the sticks I threw, but would just swim out to get them, but then drop them again, so we used to get through a lot of sticks, and eventually run out!

It struck me one day that I was now just climbing down this steep and sometimes very muddy bank, and up again, balancing without trouble whilst throwing sticks, and all in the course of a long walk, which might take over two hours. Jesse's enthusiasm spurred me on; he simply expected me to follow him down the bank, and although I found it tricky at first, I soon got used to it, and thought nothing of it. Before Jesse came into my life, I would never even have attempted such a feat, and would have been convinced that I would not be capable of it. With every walk, it seemed, my left leg was getting stronger and functioning better and my confidence in my ability to walk further and further without pain grew.

Jesse loved streams as well as rivers, and would often wander along them, nosing about and drinking the water. He also liked to roll in them, or lie flat in them if he was feeling hot in the summer, and would emerge shaking himself vigorously, ready to carry on the walk.

Walks by the river were generally a very social time for me and Jesse, and I would meet and greet people I saw regularly and Jesse would have plenty of other dogs to play with.

However, although Jesse was happy to meet and greet most people and their dogs, there were some exceptions. These were people who were dressed all in black, and people wearing hats. He was very suspicious of them, for reasons I never fully grasped, and he avoided them if at all possible, whether on a walk or on some occasion indoors.

I first realised this when we were walking along by a river, and coming the other way along the path was a family, all wearing black wetsuits. Jesse stopped dead in his tracks and started to growl at them, and then he turned away and tried to go back the way we had just come. He had never behaved like this before, and I couldn't understand what was wrong, but he flatly refused to go past them, and I had to take him via another route. As our lives together progressed, I came to realise that anyone wearing all black was in the same category of suspicion in Jesse's mind, and he always refused to have anything to do with them, and also with people wearing hats. He would often stand and bark at them, sounding quite intimidating! This never changed, despite the efforts of some kind people to reassure him and make a fuss of him. If the people wearing hats removed them, Jesse would be fine and friendly towards them again!

Jesse and the local park

When Jesse was about 2 years old, my husband and I separated. We had been married for only 8 years, but they had not been easy ones after the 'honeymoon' period had worn off. His previous wife had died of cancer, leaving him with two boys, one at Primary School and one in his teens. The family were obviously devastated by her death, and although I never met her, I was told she was a really lovely lady who had many friends and was very popular. Her husband (whom I will call Jim) could not cope at all without her, and shortly after her death we met and began going out together. I felt really sorry for the family; the two boys were white faced and withdrawn, and their father appeared to be unable to cook or look after the house or help the boys with homework, or do any of the usual domestic activities associated with family life. He had been a 'traditional' husband and had left the domestic side of family life entirely to his wife. He was also drinking excessively which the boys found frightening and made them feel insecure. It was not long before I was cleaning the house, showing him how to cook and use a washing machine correctly, and helping the younger boy with his homework.

One thing led to another, and I moved in too soon after their mother's death. The older boy became very resentful and difficult, although the younger one and I always got on really well, and he seemed much relieved to have some order in his life, and someone to care about him and help him with the considerable difficulties he faced at school, being an undiagnosed dyslexic. Gradually things went from tense to difficult, and then arguments started with and about the older boy who began to exhibit typical teenage problems, but perhaps to a greater degree than most. We did try to talk things through, but truces between us never lasted long, and more arguments ensued. Jim felt torn in his loyalties, and although he and I would have long talks about setting boundaries and being united and consistent, it never lasted, and he would soon be siding with his son against me, which made me feel upset and betrayed. He also had this curious notion that, since the boys' mother had done all the caring and disciplining of them, I should take on the same role. In vain I explained to him that he needed to be a more active parent, and that being a step-mother is a different role from being a mother, especially as the boys got older, and his older son agreed, and was very clear that I was not his mother and had no right to tell him what to do! Things became impossible in the end, and I began to dread going home after work, so I suggested to Jim that his older son, now 21, was old enough to move out and make his own way in life. Although he was very reluctant and resentful about this, for once I got my way, and he did in fact move out, started his own business and fortunately began to do well for himself.

Peace reigned in the house, for the first time, and it was into this peaceful environment that Jesse entered our lives. However, the damage had been done, and the relationship between Jim and I had been damaged irretrievably by all the arguments, and unhappiness that had gone before. We stayed together until the younger boy went to University, for his sake, and then agreed amicably to separate.

Although it was for the best, it is always difficult, I think, when a marriage breaks down, and feelings of failure and fears of loneliness are very natural. I am sure Jesse didn't miss Jim, as they never bonded, but he must have missed the younger of the two boys, as they had a great relationship, rolling around on the floor, pretend fighting and just running around together happily. Jesse's presence meant the world to me in this sad situation, as he was so affectionate, making no secret of his need for me to be around him, and I had him to care for and keep me company. Having Jesse also brought me into contact with other 'doggie people', who gave me companionship and also, in a couple of cases, turned into really close friends.

Although there is sadness in divorce, there was also, for me anyway, a great sense of release and the excitement of a new start. It was a great relief to know that I could now find my own house, in which peace and love would be paramount, and tensions and arguments would be a thing of the past. I was grateful to be able to share this new start with Jesse, and he in fact heavily influenced my choice of house, as we moved to a place which was very close to a large park which led down to the beach. It was a perfect place for both of us to live, and we very much enjoyed our time there. The park is an interesting mixture of wildlife friendly places, and more cultivated parts, with beautiful areas of wild grasses and flowers and bushes, and a series of lakes at the bottom, but also a more cultivated area which is easier to walk around. There are large grassy areas, ideal for playing ball and running around, and lots of other dogs having walks, so it was a perfect playground for Jesse and social outing for me. Jesse would enjoy playing with his ball, and with other dogs which were willing to play. He was very fast, and could outrun any dog except a whippet or a greyhound, and he enjoyed playing chase and running rings round other dogs! He also enjoyed sniffing about in the bushes and brambles, and checking out the trees for squirrels.

There were lots of rabbits in residence and foxes, which we could smell, but rarely saw. Jesse looked at the rabbits, but strangely did not seem too bothered about chasing them, until early one morning he disappeared into the bushes for a while and when I called him, he came with something in his mouth. He dropped it at my feet, and it proved to be a baby rabbit. We both stood looking at it, me wondering what to do, as he had not hurt it, but it was a long way from its mother. As I was pondering, it died of fright. Tears rolled down my cheeks as I looked at this tiny dead creature, which had never had a chance to grow up and lead a full and normal life. I didn't reproach Jesse: he was only following his instincts and doing what dogs do, but, picking up on my sorrow and understanding that he had caused it, he never took any interest in rabbits again.

Always a dog with very definite ideas, Jesse took the view that every human should have a dog with them. In the early part of his life, if he saw a person without a dog, he would immediately begin searching for the dog, and then look completely bemused if he couldn't find one! On many occasions people asked me what Jesse was doing, and I had to explain that in his view, humans and dogs went together, and a human without a dog was a strange phenomenon, and simply didn't strike him as quite right!

Generally friendly to other dogs, and always ready for a game, Jesse was not the sort of dog to be intimidated. If another dog attacked him, for whatever reason, he would get stuck in and retaliate, and he soon became a formidable fighter, although I never once saw him initiate a fight. I always broke up the fights immediately I realised it had gone beyond the growling stage, as I did not want Jesse to get hurt, or harm another dog. This involved shouting loudly and if necessary kicking the aggressor in an uncomfortable place, and it always worked well!

Unfortunately dog fights with a neighbour's dog became a serious issue. The dog was known to be aggressive, and I was warned about him when I first moved into the area. He attacked Jesse with impunity, as his owners never made the slightest effort to stop him, keep him on a lead, muzzle him, or exert any other form of control. They simply stood and watched.

I tried various strategies to overcome this problem. Initially, we simply avoided going into the park. Then this struck me as wrong, as it was a lovely place for us to walk and I had moved there partly because of its proximity. Then we tried hiding behind bushes if we saw the dog coming, but he usually found us. I spoke to the owners about trying to keep their dog under control, but to no avail. Eventually I collected signatures for a petition from other dog owners who had had similar problems to ours, with a view to presenting it to the dog warden.

In the end, it all came to a head when I saw them coming up the road out of the park, just as I was going down into it. I took Jesse up next door's drive and we hid behind the garage, but the dog had seen us and followed us, launching straight into a fight, despite my best efforts to stop him. I broke up the fight as usual, and told the owner I had had enough and was going to take action against him. I informed him I would succeed in this action because of all the signatures I had collected to support my view that his dog was a public danger and nuisance. The stream of abuse from him to me is unprintable, and was so loud and embarrassing that I suggested he might try to control himself, or walk away, as I did not want a screaming match in the street in full public view. It transpired that the last time his dog had had a fight with Jesse he had needed to take it to the vet to have bite wounds stitched up. I responded that in that case it was even more surprising that he didn't make any effort to stop his dog from fighting, and he had a duty of care to his dog as well as everyone else.

Fortunately they moved house shortly afterwards, which was a great relief, and freed many other people as well as us from an unacceptable source of anxiety on dog walks, so I never had to take action against him. I did admire Jess's courage, however. He actively avoided this dog, and did his best not to get into fights with him, but when he had no choice, he gave as good as he got, and more, it seemed!

Normally, when on walks, Jesse had his own way of approaching other dogs. He always did his 'collie creep', lying down and watching them intently and then creeping up to them, almost on his stomach, very slowly until he was nearly there, when he would suddenly bound up to them.

He would then wag his tail furiously, and encourage them to play. Very much a 'ladies man' and very good looking, he had many female friends and admirers: no hint of problems with them!

Jesse the stud dog

On one of our regular walks I became acquainted with a lady who usually had several beautiful collies with her. Jesse used to tag along as part of the pack and enjoyed being with the others, running around and playing together. She told me that she was a breeder of collies and also a show judge, and travelled all over the country, showing her own dogs and judging others. We chatted about this, and she suggested I might consider taking Jesse to dog shows, and showing him, as she thought he would do very well, as he was an excellent example of the breed. I was very flattered on Jesse's behalf, and kept quiet about his lowly heritage, making non-committal comments in response to her suggestion. In point of fact, I would hate to have gone to dog shows with Jesse, even if he had been a pedigree dog with a load of papers and a fancy name. The thought of washing and brushing and combing him, travelling sometimes quite long distances in the car and then waiting ages for our class before parading him up and down before the judges was NOT my idea of a good day out, and I was convinced Jesse would agree! However, I obviously thought it unkind to say so.

Jesse's friendship with these collies had a negative side to it, though, which I realised one day, when a dog, coming the other way, and showing signs of being nervous, was rounded on by Jesse's mates and Jesse himself, and things became quite nasty. It was the first time Jesse had ever gone up to a dog aggressively, and I was quite shocked and called him away very sharply. She also called her dogs off and no damage was done. She then explained to me about the 'pack mentality' and how a dog in a pack will be much more adventurous and less likely to respond to training than a dog on its own, and this can lead to events like we had just witnessed, where they will attack any dog which shows weakness, as indeed they would have done in the wild. I was amazed at the change in Jesse and the influence of the other dogs and quite shaken by the whole experience.

One day I met her, and having greeted each other, we had a conversation which went a bit like this:

"Jesse really is a handsome dog, isn't he? I wonder whether I might ask you to consider allowing him to be used as a sire for some of my bitches? As you know, I think he would do very well as a show dog, and I am looking for a new sire to get some new blood into my collie breeding programme. Also, I like his temperament. He is very responsive and well behaved and loyal and outgoing, and all these qualities are so important in this breed. I would imagine he could sire some excellent working dogs as well as show dogs and pets"

Jesse was indeed very good looking. He looked exactly like a Border collie, the only hint of greyhound being that his legs were a little thinner and his ears a bit smaller than one might expect. He grew a lovely long coat, which always shined, although I didn't do anything to encourage this except regular grooming and good nutrition. I made sure his weight was right for his size, so he looked in the peak of health, which he was for most of his life. He also had a lovely long tail, with a white tip, which he waved behind him like a flag. He had classic black and white collie markings, with a strip of white down his nose, a white chest and legs, and a black body. He was not only gorgeous to look at, but, as she had noted, also unusually well behaved and responsive, and I felt very proud to have him as my dog. Many people admired him, and the above request was one of several. I hesitated, but decided that the truth was the only way out of this rather awkward situation.

"Well, um, I'm sure he'd be only too happy, but he doesn't have any papers, neither does he come from a recorded line of Border Collies."

"Really? Who were his parents then, and where did you get him from?"

"Well, I got him from a farmer on the moor. He was actually the result of a mistake, a few stolen moments behind the stables, they told me, when no-one was looking, and neither of his parents had any form of pedigree. His father was a working farm dog, and his mother was well, um, actually, part greyhound!!!!"

"What do you mean? I can't see any sign of greyhound in him."

I assured her it was true, not just one of my jokes, and that Mum had not only had greyhound genes in her, but had actually looked just like a greyhound with collie markings. There was a very real chance that one or more pups might be a throwback, and turn out to be more like a greyhound than a collie, and her customers would be most upset by this! It would also do her reputation as a breeder a great deal of harm! Following an initial reaction of disbelief, the request was withdrawn, but nevertheless, Jesse and I were very flattered, and I was most amused!

Other requests were from people I met out walking, and there were about five of them in all. No-one went ahead, though, having heard the dark secret of his mixed parentage and humble background!!

However, on one occasion he himself decided to become a stud dog, and it was not quite as I might have planned or wished! On a very cold winter's day he was playing with one of his female friends on the beach. The temperature was -3 degrees, and no-one else was around. I knew the lady who owned the other dog quite well, and we chatted for a bit as the dogs played, and then went our separate ways. Only Jesse didn't. Half way along a section of beach I realised he wasn't with me, which was very unusual, so I called him but he seemed uncharactreristically reluctant to leave his doggie friend and come with me. Eventually I went back to collect him, only to discover that she was in season, and he had mated with her and was stuck inside.

Total panic! Neither I nor the bitch's owner had a clue what to do!

"Shall I try to pull him gently backwards, while you hold onto your dog?" I asked my friend, as we stood there freezing and wondering what on earth to do.

"I don't know, I suppose we could try."

"Hey! Don't do that, you could give 'em both damage to their insides. They've been having a good time, haven't they"!

This was accompanied by raucous laughter.

"What should we do then? What's happened to them?" I shouted back, naively.

Up on the promenade, a man with a Rottweiler was apparently finding this situation very amusing, and when he had finished laughing, he advised us to throw cold water over Jesse. He said it was not unusual for dogs to get stuck like that after mating, and we could wait half an hour or so, and then they would probably, but not definitely, come apart, or we could hasten the process by throwing cold water over Jesse, which would shrink his vital parts and hasten the process. How we could do this, with no containers, and only sea water available, he did not know, so we went up on the promenade, leaving the dogs, and rifled through the rubbish bins for fast food containers. After a while we found a couple and we both went in and out of the freezing sea, gathering water to throw over him to cool his ardour. Eventually they separated and we went home and dried off, hoping for the best. Apparently the bitch was right at the end of her season, and we thought it unlikely that she would conceive. However, some weeks later I was told that she was pregnant. After the initial shock, I became quite excited about this, although I worried about the responsibility of finding good homes for the pups. Unfortunately, things did not go to plan when the bitch was ready to give birth; she couldn't have them naturally and had a long difficult labour and the pups became distressed, so she had to have a caesarean.

She only had two pups. One looked very much like Jesse, with similar markings, and the other was more like his mum, who was a long legged terrier. I decided to have the one which looked like Jesse and a friend wanted the other one. Relieved that they were both going to have loving homes, we looked forward to watching them grow. The owners of the mother did everything they could to care for the pups, including staying up at night with them and encouraging them to feed, keeping them warm etc., as they were vulnerable because of the difficult birth. However, first one died, and then a few days later the other died. It was very traumatic for us all, especially the children of the terrier's owner, who were devastated. The owners of the terrier took the pups' bodies and buried them under a tree on the moor, with a little ceremony. They did not think to invite us, and I was sad, because, although Jesse was just the father, I had felt very involved because they were part of him, and I would like to have said goodbye.

In fact, I was so distressed by the whole incident that I knew I couldn't go through anything similar again, and although I had been strongly against having Jesse neutered, I changed my mind. The reasons I had not wanted him neutered were that he seemed perfect as he was, and I did not want to put him though unnecessary pain. Also I had discussed the issue with many people and it seemed that sometimes the operation can change a dog's personality, quench the life force in them a bit, and make them a bit more quiet and subdued. I did not want this for Jesse, who was so full of life and energy. Also there is the consideration that occasionally an operation will go wrong and the dog will be left maimed or, worse, die during the operation. I know this is very rare, but why take the risk when you are quite happy as you are? It was a very difficult decision, but in the end I went ahead with it. Jesse recovered quickly, it worked well, and, thank goodness, it did not change his personality in any way, or his eye for the ladies. It did, in fact, have a bonus in that he became more tolerant of other males, less likely to be picked on, and less inclined to become involved in fights.

Jesse's love of playing

All puppies are playful, and Jesse was no exception, but in his case he never grew out of it! Throughout his life he was up for any sort of game that was on offer, whether with me or with other dogs, inside or outside.

On some walks I would take a ball, and on some a Frisbee, but sometimes neither, as I did not want Jesse to become fixated on me throwing things and ignore his surroundings and other dogs. I have seen this happen to some dogs, especially Collies, and I think they miss out, especially on the chance to play and socialise with other dogs.

Jesse generally retrieved his ball with enthusiasm, and to avoid boredom, I varied the routine by bouncing it to him, or rolling it in his direction, or throwing it directly to him, all of which he greatly enjoyed. We also played a game where he was 'goalie' and I kicked the ball in his direction and he had to catch it before it went past a certain point, marked out by me.

The downside of me throwing his ball straight ahead was that when I threw it, he would arrive at the destination before the ball, even when I used a thrower, so he became bored and fed up with the lack of challenge. He had an idea, though, about how to resolve this issue, and having despaired of me improving my technique, he noted, with interest, that men, on the whole, throw balls further. Having watched carefully for a few walks, he decided to try his luck with the next man who came past carrying a ball thrower. Jesse retrieved the ball I threw for him, but instead of returning it to me, he went straight up to the man he had identified, dropped the ball at his feet, and slowly wagged his long tail, whilst grinning up at him with his most winning smile, and giving him a very appealing look from his velvet brown eyes. Unable to resist him, the man confirmed Jesse's observations by throwing the ball much further than I could have done, and giving him a chance to have a really good run. After this, Jesse made a regular habit of presenting a ball to a likely male victim, and he benefitted from some really good throws which would test his speed to the limit!

He also loved to chase after his Frisbee, but there I failed him even more, as I never got the hang of throwing it properly, despite instruction from several helpful dog owners.

The first time we saw a dog chasing a Frisbee was when we were walking along the playing fields near the office. A man with a Collie was throwing a Frisbee, and it sailed the whole length of the football pitch, with the Collie racing underneath it, and then leaping in the air to catch it as it began to come to earth. Jesse and I were equally impressed, and stopped to watch. Jesse was riveted, and could not take his eyes off this spectacle, although he was much too polite or diffident to attempt to join in. So I asked the man to show me how he did it, but although he tried several times to help me, I could not get the hang of it, and he kindly threw it a few times for Jesse before advising me to practice and going on his way!

I took his advice, and practised a great deal, but it was no use! It often didn't go very far and sometimes it would land the wrong side of a fence or hedge, in a hedge, or up a tree. Jesse was ingenious in his attempts to retrieve it, and usually managed it if it landed in the undergrowth or behind a fence, but it was trickier to get it down from a tree, and on occasion, when this happened in the park, I found the need to go home and get a ladder to retrieve it for him! However, on a walk far from home, I did another bad throw and it landed in a tree, too high up for me to reach, even with the help of a long stick. I couldn't climb the tree to get it, but Jesse refused to leave it and sat under the tree looking at it intently. Some time passed, and I was late for an appointment at work, but Jesse had made up his mind. Although generally speaking he was unfailingly co-operative and always came to call, on this occasion, he was not going anywhere without his Frisbee and nothing I said or did would shift him! Eventually a teenage lad came along, shinned up the tree and returned it to Jesse. I thanked him effusively and with much relief was to be able to get on with the day....I had begun to think we would be stuck at the tree forever!!

As well as balls and Frisbees, Jesse had a great love of soft toys. Well, of disembowelling soft toys, to be accurate. It would take him a couple of days to first play with them, then chew them, and finally remove all the stuffing. This gave him huge satisfaction, and the house would frequently look as if it had been struck by a snow storm, with stuffing lying around all over the place. Always a dog to know his own mind, he had little time for plastic or rubber toys, although sometimes he would make an exception if it squeaked! He enjoyed playing in the house with his toys, and would involve me if he could. He would bring them to me and drop them, and I would throw them to him, then he would retrieve them and start all over again. At other times he would hold onto them and refuse to give them up so I would chase him round pretending to try to get them off him. He really loved this game! Another variation was that I would tell him to stay, then go off and hide his toys round the house. He would have great fun finding them and returning them to me, wagging his tail. He was usually spot on but occasionally he brought back the wrong one, and I just laughed. It was, after all, supposed to be fun for both of us, and it always was.

A game which Jesse invented was as follows: he would put a ball or one of his toys into one or both of my wellies, usually when he knew we were just about to go for a walk, and I was getting ready, but never when I was around to see him do it. I would put my foot into the boot, encounter some strange object, shriek, and then notice Jesse beside me, grinning up at me and wagging his tail! He loved to watch my reaction at these times, and I have no doubt at all that he had a strong sense of humour.

An unusual game, but one much loved by Jesse, was eating bubbles! When I decided to have a bubble bath, Jesse would come in the bathroom with me and lie on the bath mat. He would look longingly at the bubbles, so I would offer him some in my hand. He would eat them with much relish! In fact he loved them, and they never seemed to do him any harm, so whenever I had a bubble bath, he was there, licking them off my arms, hands, knees, any part of me he could reach which had bubbles on it.

If I had a bath without bubbles he would look most disappointed, and I often added them especially to please him. Eventually he would decide he had had enough, and leave the bathroom with quiet dignity!

I was surprised to read, a few weeks ago, that someone had done some research into whether or not dogs had feelings which in any way equated to ours. I could have saved them a great deal of time and money. Any dog lover knows dogs have a range of feelings, from sadness and joy (e.g. when you leave them and return), to jealousy (if you make a fuss of other dogs, or humans get too close to you) to anger, fear, boredom, and in Jesse's case, anyway, curiosity and a great sense of humour!

As he got older, Jesse developed something of an obsession with rubber pigs which honked when he chewed them. The local pet shop offered a range of sizes and two colours, black and pink. As particular as always, Jesse decided he didn't like the biggest ones, and regarded the deep noise they made with much suspicion, but he did like the smaller ones, very much, but only the black ones and they became his favourite toy. Every so often he would de-squeak them and lose interest immediately, so I would go and buy him a new one. On one occasion, they didn't have any black ones, only pink ones, so I bought one of those instead. Jesse totally ignored it. I found this very interesting, as there is a debate about whether or not dogs see in colours, and if they do, whether they see the same colours as we do, or whether they see colours differently. The latest research suggests that dogs see only blue, yellow and grey. I don't know how good the research is, or how extensive it is, but it doesn't really account for Jesse's rejection of the pink pig! He clearly saw it as different from the black one, and had a distinct preference based on colour, as they were otherwise identical.

Cornwall

When Jesse was about 5 years old, I met and got to know a man who became my new partner. I was very busy at the time, with work during the week, and playing the organ on Sundays, so the easiest way to spend time together was for him to come and stay with me, since he was retired. This he did on a regular basis for about 6 months, usually spending several days of each week with Jesse and me. We seemed to have much in common, and one of the interests which attracted us to each other was a love of dogs and the countryside. He also had a Border collie, and I was pleased that Jesse would have a friend and companion as well. She proved to be less of a companion for him than I had hoped, though, because although she was great with people, including children, she was quite aggressive towards other dogs. However, she and Jesse managed to get along well enough when she visited our house with her owner (whom I will call Bob), as Jesse loved female dogs and was very friendly towards her, and she respected his space to a degree. Bob and I got on very well, and shared a love of books, good food and wine, walking, music and conversation as well as both having a strong sense of humour, that had us reeling with laughter a lot of the time. It seems to me that when people fall in love, they are so excited and happy that even the smallest things seem funny, and I remember that, both being rather absent minded, we would frequently forget where we had parked the car, if we left it in a large car park. We would first of all try to remember, and disagree about exactly where we had left it, and then end up searching the entire park, until one of us would find it, and signal triumphantly to the other, shaking with laughter at our incompetence!

Eventually it got to the point when we wanted to be together all the time, in the hope that our relationship would prove to be long term. This caused me quite a lot of heart searching, as he wanted me to move to Cornwall where he lived with a lodger and two of his three adult children. The two 'children' were in fact at University, but they both returned for all of the holidays, and were very fond of Cornwall. This was especially true of his daughter, who had 3 ponies which she kept near their house there. I had recently left my lovely interesting job, because the Senior Management had decided that it would be cheaper if I was office based, and if the people I had visited around the county communicated with me via the Internet. I could still run seminars, but then would have to send students tasks and questions to which they would have to respond in writing. I didn't agree with this approach and for me it would have meant no more visits, no more laughs and socialising, having to sit still all day in a large open plan office (which I find quite impossible) and worst of all, having to leave Jesse at home.

So I left. My intention was to get another job, which I had lined up, which would only have been part time, and therefore would have allowed me to spend more time playing and singing music and with Jesse.

However, an alternative to this plan was to move to Cornwall. There were a couple of snags, however. One was that I was very happy at the church at which I played, which I would have to leave, and worse, I would have to leave my friends and the life Jesse and I had made for ourselves, which we both enjoyed.

Another complication was that Cornwall is quite remote, and it would take me a lot further away from my grown up children, who lived in a city which was only an hour and a half's drive away from where I currently lived and whom I saw quite frequently.

Anyway, after much heart searching and discussion, I decided to make the break and go to Cornwall, on the condition that my partner and I would both return to my house (all being well) when the 'children' had finished their University courses, and no longer needed a parental home to return to during the holidays. My partner agreed to this, and although I left behind a number of upset people, I felt it was worth it. The one thing I would not leave behind, though, was my beloved Gospel Choir. Although it would mean a lot of travelling, I was prepared to do it. I think having Jesse helped me to make the decision to move to Cornwall. At least I knew he would be with me, and I would have the security of his love amongst all the unknown things to come.

Cornwall is well known for its beauty and its wildlife, and wonderful unspoilt beaches and coves, and in many ways it was a beautiful place to live. Bob's house stood on the top of a cliff and had amazing sea views and ready access to a lovely sandy cove and cliff walks in both directions. Although one needs to be fit and energetic to negotiate the steep cliffs which the walks entail, they are beautiful, with lovely views, very pretty wild flowers, and lots of space for dogs to run around. My left leg was by now perfectly able to negotiate the cliffs so posed no problems for me. Jesse loved these walks and beaches, and the freedom they gave him, and he and my partner's dog (which I will call Bess), would race each other, and have a wonderful time together. Bess was a real sea dog, and she would go fearlessly into the roughest of seas, and lie down with waves crashing over her, waiting for a ball or stick to be thrown in for her to chase. On these occasions Jesse looked on in admiration, but took care not to join in! Bess was completely undeterred, however, and would vanish under the waves, only to pop up again like a cork when they had passed!

To his delight, Jesse found flocks of finches on the cliffs and in the fields just behind them, and had a wonderful time chasing them for miles.

The first time this happened, we were walking along the cliff top with Bob and Bess. There were a lot of fields behind the cliff top, separated only by gates and hedges. Jesse was overjoyed to notice a flock of finches overhead. They were the first he had seen in Cornwall, and he was very excited to realise that he could run with them there as well as at home. He stopped and watched them intently. Then he started gently bouncing up and down, preparing for a run. Bob stopped as well and stared at him, completely bemused.

"What on earth is Jesse doing?" he asked.

"Well, he's looking at that flock of finches flying overhead" I said, anticipating what Jesse's next move would be, but not wanting to give the game away just yet.

"What's so special about that?" demanded Bob, "they often fly round here."

"Just wait and see", I replied.

Then Jesse exploded into action, barking excitedly as he always did. He ran underneath the flock, which keep swooping down just above his head and then flying up way out of reach. Over the five barred gate he flew, through the hedge, as if it wasn't there and away, out of sight, and soon out of earshot.

Bob was amazed and concerned, and Bess watched with interest, showing no desire to join in with Jesse.

"Do something, Diane, call him back, we have no idea where he is! Aren't you worried, he could be anywhere!" said Bob. "How can you let him just run off like that? Why is he chasing them, he must know he'll never catch them?"

"Oh, he doesn't want to catch them", I replied. "He just can't resist running with them. No need to call him, he'll be back soon".

This was too much for Bob and completely outside his experience! In vain he took it into his own hands and stood there, calling Jesse. Even if Jesse had heard him, which I doubt, he would have taken no notice. As I have said before, Jesse didn't like being told what to do, and only listened to me because of the love between us. He never took any notice of anyone else.

I just carried on walking and eventually Bess joined me. Bob stood at the spot where Jesse had disappeared.

"Don't walk on, he won't know where we are when he finally decides to come back, and then he'll get lost!"

"Oh no, he will know where we are, he always does," I replied airily, and sure enough, a few minutes later Jesse appeared , panting but so delighted to have found his beloved flocks of finches once again. He just joined us and settled down to walk with us as if nothing had happened. Bess regarded him as some kind of crazy idiot, and never attempted to join him on these expeditions, which became a regular feature of our Cornwall walks, but Jesse didn't care, he was in his element!

The part of Cornwall in which Bob lived was full of all sorts of walks, not just confined to the sea and the cliffs. There were walks through farmland, woods and fields as well as by the sea, and Jesse and I could find loads of variation and had lots of discovering to do. Because Bob would never take his dog to the start of a walk in the car, but would only do walks from home, Jesse and I discovered a lot of new walks by ourselves and really enjoyed being alone together again.

The ponies which Bob's daughter kept were an added interest, as I have kept ponies and horses for a lot of my life, and my children were very enthusiastic riders, so I ended up looking after the daughter's ponies while she was away at University, and riding one of them on a regular basis. Bess was wary of the ponies, but Jesse loved them, and he and I would set out together for a ride. He needed no training to accompany a pony, and, as usual, just had a sense of what was expected. He always trotted to heel on the roads and lanes, but once we were on a bridle path or open field and could move on to a faster pace he would gallop alongside with the greatest joy and enthusiasm, never getting in the way of the pony, but hugely enjoying the speed and the distance which rides enabled us to cover.

He was not so keen on the electric fence which divided the field, however, because one day he made the mistake of putting his nose on it. I had just moved it and switched it on, and I think he was interested in the clicking noise it made when it was active. Having put his nose too close to it, he received a shock and shot off across the field in horror! He was reluctant to come into the field for about 2 weeks after that, and even when he relented and came back in with me, he gave the fence a very wide berth!

The farrier's visit was another matter, however. When farriers cut back horses' feet, the trimmings are very tasty for dogs, and both Bess and Jesse would be lying in wait when the farrier came to the field to trim the ponies' hooves, and replace their shoes. The dogs would vie with each other, trying to be the first to grab a piece of hoof as it came down from the farrier's knife! No fear of ponies or electric fences operated then!

Bess and Jesse seemed to get on quite well, on the whole, but only because Jesse accepted her status as top dog. She was quite unkind to him, taking his toys, lying in his bed, growling at him in the car, and always having to go first on a narrow path or through the front door. This must have been slowly getting on his nerves, although he didn't show it, because one day he just lost his temper entirely, and went for her with a frightening ferocity. He was younger, bigger and stronger than she was, and a very accomplished fighter. I should perhaps have left them to sort it out once and for all, but I was afraid he might really hurt her or even kill her, so I called him off. He never fought her again, or even growled at her, but I sometimes wondered whether I had done the right thing, as she continued to bully him for some time. Eventually things settled down, and they rubbed along together pretty well.

When we arrived in Cornwall I soon realised that my partner and I had somewhat different ideas about how to treat a dog. One evening, shortly after my arrival in January, we walked along the cliff path, with the dogs, to a local hotel for a drink and a meal. It was very windy, cold and wet, and when we got there, he proceeded to tie his dog up outside. I was quite shocked, as it had never crossed my mind that the dogs wouldn't be coming in with us, and I flatly refused to leave Jesse outside in that weather (or in any weather for that matter). After an argument with Bob, I went in and asked permission to take the dogs inside, and it turned out that they were welcome in the bar, which resolved the problem. My position was always that if a pub or hotel did not want dogs, I did not want to be in it!

We also had an unfortunate incident in which I left Jesse in his care when I went shopping, and returned to find no sign of him. Jesse always greeted me with huge enthusiasm when I returned home, and his absence threw me straight into panic mode. I asked Bob where he was. Bob didn't know. I rushed round the house and garden, frantically calling him, but there was no sign of him and no sound. Eventually in desperation, I looked in the garage, which adjoined the kitchen. There he was, shut in, in the dark, and over the moon to see me and be rescued. Taking a leaf from Jesse's book, and trying to be loving and accepting, I hid my anger, and asked Bob calmly how Jesse could have come to be in there. He just said nonchalantly that he had gone in for something, and Jesse must have followed him, and he didn't notice and so had inadvertently shut him in. I asked him if he could try and check next time, as it must have been horrible for Jesse to be shut in a cold damp garage with nothing to lie on, just a lot of junk lying around, for what was quite a long time. Bob didn't seem to fully understand my concerns and made no comment. It happened again a few weeks later, so after that I never left Jesse alone with him. If I couldn't take him wherever I was going, I would just leave him in the car, for as short a time as possible.

I also found that I walked Jesse much more often than he walked Bess, so soon I took both dogs with me, and they enjoyed being together, splashing about in streams and racing along the cliffs and beach. They both became very good in the narrow country lanes, and would immediately stop close to the hedge when they heard a car coming, and stay there until it had passed. Often they heard a car coming before I did, and I only knew a car was coming because they had positioned themselves close to the hedge and were waiting. Neither needed a lead for walks of his nature. Bess was very well bred, and came from a line of dogs which were trained for sheep dog trials and competitions. On walks she would rush ahead and out to the side, and then crouch down. This is what dogs do in sheepdog trials, and once crouched down beside a flock of sheep they await the handler's instructions. In Bess's case, since there were not any sheep, a ball had to take their place, but again, as with Jesse, it showed how strong these genes are which are bred into working collies, as she had received no training in sheep herding either.

I took this opportunity of our walks without Bob to train Bess to be less aggressive towards other dogs, as I heard from people who lived in the village that she was regarded as a menace by a lot of dog owners, and they had to deviate in their walks to avoid her. It took a while, but a few months later she had fully grasped that being aggressive towards other dogs was a bad idea, and life became much easier for us all. She had a very nasty skin condition, which caused her to scratch and bleed and did not respond to anything the vet gave her, or the nappy rash cream her owners put on her and her coat was badly matted through lack of grooming (she was long haired, like Jesse). It occurred to me that she probably had an allergy so I started by changing her diet and avoiding any cereals. It worked like a dream and the rash disappeared and the scratching stopped. Next was the grooming. She disliked this and was aggressive at first, which was why they had avoided grooming her in the first place, but gradually by patience and kindness and making sure I was gentle, I persuaded her to accept being brushed and her coat started gleaming like Jesse's and she looked great. It probably helped her to feel less aggressive, as anyone who has experienced any kind of skin condition knows how annoying it is and how grumpy it makes you feel, so being free of it must have made her a great deal happier.

Although we had some wonderful walks and some happy times together, I found the move to Cornwall much more difficult than I had anticipated. I had not intended to retire, and was in fact too young to retire, but didn't see the point of looking for a job just for the 18 months I had agreed to live there, and had had rosy visions of Bob and I spending lots of time together and me getting a good organist's post and singing in local choirs. But it wasn't quite like that. Like many people when they first stop work, I found it incredibly difficult, as I had not only enjoyed my job, but everything that goes with it; the structure it provides, the sense of purpose, the independence, self respect, identity, and earning money. All that was gone and it left a huge void in my life. Just being at home with each day stretching out before me was a huge adjustment. Bob had been retired for a few years, and had fully adjusted, and was greatly enjoying the slower pace of life this entailed, having retired early because of stress, but I hated it. I hated getting up late and having a leisurely breakfast before taking the dogs out and having a coffee on the way home, a 'little rest' after lunch, and pottering around, it just wasn't me at all, and this caused conflict. I really did try to adjust, again thinking of Jesse and how he had adapted himself to my way of life, but I just couldn't. I also missed my life and friends and colleagues back home more than I had ever anticipated, and even more, I missed my children, of whom I now saw a lot less.

I decided to be constructive and carve out a life for myself, but it took a while to work out how. Bob had managed to discover a life style that suited him well, as he had a voluntary job driving people to hospital appointments and back home, and also sang with two male voice choirs. He had a friend he met regularly for a drink in the pub, and belonged to another singing group that met in the local pub on a monthly basis. So although his pace of life was leisurely, he did have some purpose and interest in it. He also took on consultancy work commissions from time to time.

Unfortunately, our joint interest in music became a dividing factor between us, as Cornwall is full of Male Voice choirs, but there is very little in the way of choirs for women or mixed choirs. In fairness, he did eventually find us a mixed choir in which we could both sing, but I hated the type of music they sang, and it was really a choir for inexperienced singers, and held little challenge for me. It was always followed by a session in the pub, which didn't really interest me, and meant getting home late and leaving Jesse for quite a long time albeit with Bess and the lodger. I stuck with it for 6 months, but then had to confess how much I disliked it, and, although Bob was annoyed, he did agree that we didn't have to keep going!

Prior to my going to Cornwall, Bob had told me that there were plenty of vacancies for organists in the area. This was in fact true, but only of the less good organs in the smaller churches. All the good jobs were taken! Although this was disappointing, I made the best of it by joining a team of organists who played at four small churches which were linked together in a 'Mission Community' with the same Vicar. All the organs were pretty awful but some were better than others. All the churches welcomed Jesse, however, and made a great fuss of him, no problems on that score! I was slightly taken aback to be told:

"I hope you don't mind, dear, but we only pay our male organists here, you know, they have families to keep..."

Cornwall had clearly missed out on the Equalities Act in 2010, not to mention the Equal Pay Act of 1976, but Cornwall is in many ways a law unto itself! Words failed me, but no-one plays in a church for much money anyway, so I accepted the status quo! Thanks to Jesse's influence, I was becoming more accepting of situations I didn't really like, and instead of feeling put down by this, I just thought,

"I want to play the organ, they want me to do it; I am not short of money, since I have rented out my house and have the income from that, so just let things be". So that's what I did.

We had one incident at one of the churches which was particularly unfortunate. There was to be a christening and lots of family and friends arrived. I was playing quiet music before the service, and suddenly the power went off! You can't play an organ without electricity, as the air needs to be pumped into the organ pipes for it to be able to make the notes sound, so playing the organ was not an option. Power cuts were not unusual in that part of Cornwall, but in this case the timing was appalling! The Vicar suggested I might play the piano which was present in the church, but any musician who has spent time in churches will know that almost every church has a piano, kindly donated by someone who doesn't want it anymore, because it is not a good piano, and that these are never played or tuned. My heart sank to my boots when I opened the lid, to discover that about a quarter of the keys were actually missing. It was of course, hopelessly out of tune. I explained to the Vicar that to try to play this was actually worse than having no music at all, and I was happy to lead the singing of the hymns without an instrument, but she would not be moved, so I did my best and made the most appalling noise on this dreadful instrument. No-one said anything, but the day for the people at the baptism must have been quite marred by this awful music; worse, for my ego anyway, was the fear that they suspected me of being quite unable to play!!

Unfortunately, despite my efforts to make the best of a bad situation, I was feeling very cut off musically, and felt a real need to be involved in music of a kind that I enjoyed and was used to.

I decided to start my own church choir, with members drawn from all 4 churches in which I played (and later on a few who didn't go to church at all) and it became a quite successful four part mixed choir and grew to a respectable size with about 3 or 4 to a part. We sang a variety of music, but mainly church music aimed at Christmas and Easter and other church festivals. To my surprise we were asked to go and sing at the opening of a local Art Gallery. This was quite an honour for a small recently formed choir, so we practised really hard, so that we could provide entertainment comprising of half an hour of light and varied music for people to listen to as they browsed around. We were all quite excited when the day came, but in the end, nobody at all turned up and the place was entirely empty, except for us and the owner of the gallery, and remained so throughout!! It is the one and only time this has happened to me, and I was a bit lost as to what to do. The owner of the Art Gallery, despite being bitterly disappointed herself, saved the day.

"You can sing to me", she said firmly, and, getting herself a chair, she sat down in front of us. So we did and she applauded after every song. It was a really weird experience, singing to an audience of one, but then, Cornwall was full of the unexpected!

I then discovered, to my delight, that there was a voluntary Cathedral Choir at Truro. These choirs stand in for the professional Cathedral choir as required, but also do performances and stand on their own as good quality choirs in their own right. I went on the website, and discovered that they were currently auditioning for Sopranos. Nervously, I went along. The audition was more like a singing lesson than an audition, with the choir master explaining to me how to improve the way I sang, using a variety of techniques. Convinced that I had not made the grade, I nevertheless waited anxiously for the result. Nothing came through on my email for ages, and six weeks later, I decided that I had obviously not made the grade. However, eventually I heard that I had indeed been accepted! It was a brilliant choir, he was a brilliant musician, and I loved every second of singing with them. Then a very young man, but a very talented musician, he is now the Assistant Organist at Windsor, and played for the wedding of Prince Harry and Megan!!

The St. Mary's Voluntary Cathedral choir really was the highlight of my time in Cornwall, along with the wonderful walks that Jesse and I enjoyed together and with Bess.

Unfortunately I had had to give up running the Gospel Choir. The journey proved to be longer and more exhausting than I had anticipated, as well as expensive on petrol. The final straw came when Bob's daughter had given Jesse a bone a couple of days before I was due to run a Gospel Choir practice. Although he had been enthusiastic about it, unfortunately it hadn't agreed with him and he had been quite ill the previous day. I had thought he had completely recovered but sadly he had not. During choir practice he kept running to the door, asking to go out, but I had been so preoccupied I had not noticed. He had awful diarrhoea all over the carpet when he could hold it in no longer. Most of the choir were sympathetic , but one lady, who disliked me, and was keen to run the choir herself, made a huge fuss and reported this to the Vicar, who said it might be better if I left Jesse at home in future, even though we had cleared up the mess and there was no staining of any kind. There was no way I was going without Jesse, so that was the end of that.

Still rather under occupied, I hit on the idea of playing the piano at Residential Homes. I didn't charge them, but thought they might like it if I played light classical music of a gentle and calming nature for an hour or so a week. Several homes jumped at the chance, and so I began to visit them, five of them, once a week, and Jesse, of course, came with me. The residents liked Jesse, but he was very wary of them at first, especially in homes where some residents had dementia, and although he accompanied me to four of the five, the fifth one was too much for him, as it was very noisy, since people with dementia can easily get disoriented and aggressive and arguments were not uncommon while the music was going on. It soon became clear that the residents in all the homes preferred popular music to which they could sing along, to my light classics, so I learned a new repertoire of music, largely from the '40s and '50s, which was well received.

I discovered that there was a huge difference between private homes and local authority homes. The private homes were smaller, better staffed, much friendlier, and had residents who needed support, but were still capable of conversation, and doing some activities independently. After I had finished playing I would stop and have tea and a conversation with them, and learned a lot about their lives, and especially about the years of the Second World War. At one home, there was a man who had been a farmer, and he used to love Jesse coming in. Jesse was fine with him, and he would reminisce about his farming days and his working collies, and take a great interest in Jesse and the way the behaved in certain situations and compare him to the dogs he used to own, and comment on the difference between Jesse's life and his dogs' working lives. There was a lady in the same home, who remembered songs she used to sing at school, and soon we were digging out traditional folk songs and sea shanties to add to the repertoire.

However, the Local Authority homes were very different. On the whole, the residents were less able than in the private homes and in many cases their major health problem was Alzheimer's or Dementia. It struck me as an incredibly sad disease, as some of the residents would get terribly distressed at things that were going on in their minds, which bore no relation to what was happening around them, and they found it hard to explain the cause of their distress, or to overcome it. Others would become aggressive, as the inhibitors in the brain degenerated, and there were frequently loud arguments going on as I was trying to play.

When I went in one week, a man was arguing with Care staff. He had just come into the home, and was completely disoriented. He had been a farmer, and he became most upset when he realised he hadn't just come for a visit (as his family had probably told him, in order to get him there). He explained repeatedly that he had to get back to the farm as it was milking time and the cows would be waiting and there was no-one else to do it. Nothing anyone said would convince him that someone else was now looking after the cows and he became increasingly agitated. In the end the staff had to physically restrain him from leaving and trying to get back to the farm, which was probably being run by another family member, or had been sold on.

One very moving incident was when I set up my electronic piano next to a man who was very ill, and lay, comatose, on a bed in the living area, having to be fed though a straw. He never moved, or showed any signs of life at all in my presence and I wanted to see whether I could get any reaction from him, thinking he might be more aware of me if I was right next to him. After a while, I heard him, very faintly, beginning to sing. He opened his eyes, and continued to join in for a short while before slipping away again. It was a rare moment of consciousness for him, and, I hope, a happy one.

Another moving incident was at Christmas, when carols were required, and I wrote out the words of familiar carols in large print and gave them to the residents, but they didn't really need them, as they could remember the words. It is certainly true that when people become very old, and memory starts to fail, it is the long term memory that survives the best, and is in the sharpest focus. We sang carols for an hour, me taking requests, and although we didn't all sing the same carol at the same time, there was a convivial atmosphere. As I left I heard them still singing, all singing different carols at the same time, oblivious to the discord, but happy in their memories and their own worlds.

Every home I visited had good walks nearby, so on the way home Jesse and I would stop off and try a new walk. Jesse soon got the hang of jumping over Cornish styles, and five barred gates if necessary, and we often set out following a 'public footpath' sign, with no idea at all where we were going to end up. Generally we found our way back, but we had a few scary moments when we got completely lost. Fortunately Jesse had a better sense of direction than me, and if I was unsure where to go, I would leave it to him, and usually he was spot on.

One day I suggested to Bob that he and Bess might like to join us on one of our newly discovered walks, which I thought we would all enjoy, and was nearby. He agreed, but after a few minutes he said he already knew the walk, and had done it before. Disappointed but undeterred, I carried on, but at a junction where Jesse and I had previously turned right, he disagreed and said it was better to turn left. I deferred to his judgement, but pointed out that I would then not know where I was going, since I had never been that way before, so would have to rely on his knowledge. He assured me that he knew the way, so we continued on ....and on, and on. Eventually we came to a road, and it was quite clear that he had absolutely no idea where we were. He kept asking me which way to go, but, as I had explained earlier, I had no idea either, as I would have gone the other way in the first place. After more than two hours, I was getting really tired and fed up, and neither of us knew where we were, although we were by now back walking in fields. Although my left leg had improved immeasurably through my long walks with Jesse, it still had a limit before it started to hurt and swell and we were getting dangerously near that limit.

"Let's walk up to the top of the hill over there and see whether we can get our bearings" he said. I told him that quite honestly, I couldn't face climbing a hill just at that moment and asked if he would go and have a look and communicate to me what, if anything, he had found out about our whereabouts. He agreed to this, and went off, while I sat and waited. Both the dogs ran to and fro between us, getting quite distressed, as collies can't cope when people set out together and then split up, since their herding instinct is so strong that they want the 'flock' to stay together. Eventually, however, they both stayed with me. There was no sign of Bob at all, and after what seemed like an eternity, I got up and took the dogs along some tractor tracks, which I had wanted to do in the first place, the reasoning being that it was likely to lead us to a barn or a farm which would help us identify where we were. Whilst we were on our way, I received a text from Bob.

"I am back at the car now" it said. No directions, no explanations, nothing at all to help us find our way. Fortunately my reasoning had proved correct, and indeed the tractor tracks led us to a farm which I recognised, and from which we could find out way back, but I was not very happy.

An argument ensued when I tried to explain calmly and reasonably that I had become exhausted and quite frightened towards the end of the walk, and I didn't understand why he hadn't helped us to find our way back, when he had found it. He became angry, as he always did when he felt he was being criticised, and unfortunately this was not the first argument of this nature we had had. Things were slowly unravelling between us, however much I tried to be unfailingly kind and reasonable, and not for the first time, he refused to speak to me for two days afterwards.

I felt very upset at this prolonged estrangement, especially after everything I had given up to join him in Cornwall, and I felt very isolated socially, with no friends or family around. If it hadn't been for Jesse, I don't know what I would have done, as I had rented my house out, and had nowhere to go, except to impose on friends and family, which would have been difficult for any length of time. Jesse's steadfast and intense love for me had always been a big support, but never more so than when we were in Cornwall.

Things were also difficult with Bob's son and daughter. His son appeared to have a serious drink problem, which led to conflict between him and his father, and certainly didn't make my life any easier. Having experienced this type of situation before, I kept out of all arguments and made no comment, but I began to dread the times when he decided to come home. His daughter was friendly to me at first, but as time went by she changed towards me, I don't know why. I think she felt I was taking her father away, and trying to take her mother's place, and she said it didn't feel like her home any more. It must have been difficult for her, seeing another woman living in their family home after her mother had left, very unexpectedly, about a year before, but we were not able to discuss it.

In any event, there were a lot of stresses and strains developing, and the early months of romantic love were becoming a distant memory. Things came to a head when Bob's daughter tried to insist that we stayed on in the house in Cornwall after she had graduated, so she could come and live with us there. In vain I explained to both of them that the chances of her getting a good job using her degree in such a remote part of the country were non-existent, and she really did need to leave home and find a proper job, worthy of her education, ability and age (she was 23 by this time, coming up to 24). In the end, I simply said I was going to return home as originally agreed, and he must do what he decided was best for him and his daughter.

Back Home

So that's what I did.

It was wonderful to be back in my own home, after the strain of living in someone else's house, a life-style I didn't enjoy, and being in a relationship which was beginning to unravel, complicated by two adult children in their 20s behaving more like teenagers. I think Jesse enjoyed it too, just the two of us again, and peace and quiet and contentment surrounding us.

After a while, though, Bob decided to join us, hoping a new start without all the family 'baggage' would make things better between us. His ex-wife bought him out of the house so that she could let their daughter live there, but, of course, in the event, the daughter found a job, initially in London and then abroad, so the house, as far as I know, was left empty except for occasional family visits.

Just as I had found it hard to settle in Cornwall, so Bob found it hard to settle with me, and live in my house. He was reluctant to get involved in local life, but unable to explain why, and as the relationship slowly deteriorated further, life became very difficult for both of us and the dogs, who were the innocent victims of this human drama. Dogs are very sensitive to atmosphere, and it can't have been easy for either of them. Jesse continued to love and support me and mop up my tears, and I continued to give him as good a life as possible. Eventually, Bob decided to leave, and return to London, where he had lived for most of his life. I felt nothing but relief. Jesse and I saw him and Bess off, looking forward to resuming our peaceful lives together, although it was still a sad end to an episode which had started with such hope and excitement.

It always surprises me that people think dogs, as a species, are inferior to humans. They are very different, of course, and their intellectual capacity far less well developed than ours, but they do have abilities which we either never had or have lost through the evolutionary process. There are many examples from Jesse's life. One was the way he always knew when I was upset, even if I tried to hide it, and would comfort me and stay near me. Another was the way he always knew where we were when he was chasing birds and could join us from some distance away. Jesse hated thunder, and he always knew long before I did if a storm was brewing, and would show signs of clinginess and anxiety.

Often you hear stories of dogs who know when their human is expected home from work, and will wait regularly and expectantly at the right time. Dogs have a capacity for living in the present, and enjoying the moment, which I think is enviable, and we humans rarely have. They have a wonderful ability to forgive, although they rarely forget, and to accept people as they are, without resentment, retaliation or aggression, even if they are treated badly. There was so much I could learn from Jesse, and so much we could all learn from most domesticated dogs. They know which strangers like dogs and which don't, although we would not necessarily be able to guess from the stranger's body language. Their amazing sense of smell enables us to enlist their help for things like sniffing out drugs, bombs, and more recently, cancer. Their willingness to commit themselves to people with disabilities and to be their eyes and/or ears, with loyalty and faithfulness, even though it restricts their own lives, without any apparent resentment, is something we would be lucky to find in humans. They are content to live simply, and ask only for food, exercise and company, unlike us who are consumers on a ridiculous and highly damaging scale.

Above all, the misdemeanours which they commit, unless they have been very screwed up by human ill treatment, are pretty minor; like not coming to call or obeying other commands, or chasing cats or making a mess in the house. It is rare to see a dog attacking a human or another dog so viciously that they do serious damage, unless they have been trained by humans to do so, whereas sadly this happens all too often with humans.

Unlike us, dogs, on the whole, accept each other, even if some are friendlier than others; serious fights between them are rare. Jesse and Bess were a good example of this. Although they wouldn't have chosen to live together, they accepted it, and learned a way of being which was positive and involved them having a good time together, especially on walks. In contrast, Bob and I did choose to live together but in the end couldn't manage to do so happily and with love and acceptance.

When you compare dogs' misdemeanours with some of ours, including child and animal abuse, rape, murder, genocide, and the manufacture of increasingly dangerous weapons, to say nothing of driving other species to extinction and trashing the planet by global warming and the excessive use of plastic, dogs seem to be to be far and away the less destructive of the two species!

Jesse and small children

My story has painted a picture of a dog who was not only good looking, but exceptionally intelligent, intuitive and loving, whilst at the same time being very much his own person and great fun to be with. All this is true, but none of us is perfect, and Jesse was no exception. There were two areas in his life in which he really struggled. One of them was being with young children. In a way, it didn't affect us much, as there were no young children in our lives, and generally speaking we walked in remote areas where there were not small children around, but occasionally it caused problems in the town in the summer.

However everything changed when my son announced, out of the blue, that he and his partner were going to have a baby. This was exciting news for them both, and when the baby was a few weeks old, my son came to stay for a long week-end with the baby, while his partner was away. Jesse was fine, and I sat quite happily with the baby on my knee, stroking Jesse at the same time, to avoid any jealousy. The week-end was relaxed and no problems emerged between Jesse and the baby, in whom Jesse showed mild interest.

As time went on, and the baby began to crawl and then became a toddler, things changed and visits from my son and grandson became more difficult as unfortunately, Jesse began to look intently at the toddler, showing signs of unease and anxiety. Between visits, I spent a long time with Jesse at playgrounds, where he could see toddlers playing, from the safety of our position behind a fence, in the hope that he would get used to them, and realise they were not a threat to him. A few parents were willing to let him meet their children slowly, in a non threatening manner, in order to show him that there was nothing to fear, but although he reluctantly co-operated with this and did not show signs of aggression towards them, sadly, he never really got used to them, and was always uneasy around them. Eventually, I had to ask parents of children under 5 not to let their children approach Jesse and stroke him, as I knew he found it difficult and stressful.

Left to himself, Jesse treated children a he treated adults he didn't like, and simply ignored them. He never, ever made an aggressive move towards them if they were just walking by or playing, but because he was a very attractive 'fluffy' dog, a lot of children wanted to stroke him, and occasionally some would rush up to him and try to grab hold of him, which would make him bare his teeth and growl. My worst nightmare was that one day he would snap at a child, and injure them in some way, if I was not quick enough to intercept them in the absence of their parents. Most parents tell their children not to rush up to strange dogs, but to ask first whether it is OK, but unfortunately, some do not, and some children do not obey parents. The only way to avoid children was to avoid going into the town or on the beach for the whole Easter to October period, which seemed too much to ask, especially as Jesse was no danger to children unless they actively flung themselves on him, so I was not unduly concerned, although always alert.

And then out of the blue, we found ourselves in the sort of situation I had been hoping would never happen! The town was unusually crowded, and normally I would have avoided it, but walking Jesse on the 'dogs only' part of the beach one day, I was suddenly desperate for the toilet. We speeded onto the green where the toilets were located, only to find a long queue outside them. Worse, there was a newly erected sign saying 'NO DOGS ALLOWED IN THE TOILETS'. This created something of quandary for me, as I was on my own with him. I could not possibly leave Jesse alone outside, as the area was teeming with small children, but neither could I wait for the toilet until I got home. As I was standing there wondering what I should do, a small girl of about three hurtled alone out of the Ladies, and seeing Jesse, flung herself on him, shouting:

"Oh what a lovely fluffy dog," at the top of her voice. Her slightly older brother emerged from the Gents in time to see Jesse snap at her and to hear her terrified screams. He bore her off into the crowds, and I went to the front of the queue, and explained the problem to the attendant, who very kindly let me in with Jesse immediately, so I could get out of this difficult situation. When we emerged, a very muscular man arrived, covered in tattoos, with both children beside him. He was very angry and the little girl was still crying.

"Did your dog do this?" he shouted, loudly, and lifted her T shirt to reveal a red mark, but, thank goodness, no broken skin.

"Yes", I said, bravely, and explained the situation, and how Jesse and I were both taken by surprise by her actions, and there was no time to stop her from flinging herself on top of him. Although I felt a strong urge to defend Jesse's actions, I did not point out that it might have been better if she had been accompanied into the Ladies at her age, nor that she should have been warned not to approach strange dogs in this way, as I felt it would be best to try to calm things down, rather than risk inflaming them. I told him that although Jesse was anxious around young children, he had never snapped at a child before, and apologised profusely for his behaviour.

At this he calmed down, and agreed no serious damage had been done, and after saying that she shouldn't really have put us in that position as she had been told not to rush up to strange dogs, he left amicably enough.

However, it was a horrible experience for all of us, and I could never let Jesse get near small children again, as he obviously just could not cope with them. It is unfortunately true that although often a dog snaps because of the behaviour of humans towards them, they always get the blame, and I was really worried about this inability of Jesse's to tolerate small children, fearing it could result in a very nasty situation arising. I think that had I seen my grandson more often, Jesse might have become used to him, as I have seen many Collies happily playing with children, or being part of a family group, but my son lived far enough away for me not to see a great deal of him, and certainly not enough for Jesse to become used to the child. When they did come to visit, my son and his partner were very anxious about the safety of their son with Jesse in the vicinity, and I think their anxiety, although understandable, contributed to his sense of unease and validated it in his mind. One grandchild became two, and then my daughter produced two children, quite close together in age, and Jesse's dislike of children meant that we always had to keep them apart, which was an unfortunate complication. The outcome was that I had to visit them, and leave Jesse behind, rather than them visiting me.

I never really got to the bottom of why Jesse found small children so hard to cope with. I think it was their sudden unpredictable movements and the sheer noise of them shouting and crying that he couldn't bear. Maybe it was his sheepdog instincts, which told him that that sudden movements meant a sheep breaking away from the flock, and he needed to be alert and ready for action. Maybe it was just the noise levels, and the fear that they might grab him at any minute, as many of them tried to, but whatever it was, nothing would persuade him that they were not a threat to him, and he never learned to relax in their presence.

Luckily, when I went to see the grandchildren, I was able to leave Jesse with some friends. He was not the sort of dog to stay happily with dog minders, and I was very grateful that these friends were willing to look after him from time to time. They were close friends, so we saw a great deal of each other, which meant Jesse was happy to be left with them, although he was always very pleased to see me when I returned. They had various dogs, during Jesse's life time, and often looked after other peoples' dogs, so Jesse had plenty of friends to play with, which he enjoyed. The rules of the house were quite different from mine: dogs were allowed on sofas and beds, and there was a very relaxed atmosphere, and occasionally an element of chaos going on!

My friends called Jesse "The Perfect One" (PO for short), as he was so well behaved, in and out of the house, and they said he enjoyed letting his hair down and chilling out when he went to stay with them!

I don't know how he felt about it, but he moved with ease between their household and mine, with our different expectations of him, and fitted into each happily.

Jesse and Vets

The other problem Jesse had was that he simply could not cope with vets. Although he may have been nicknamed 'P.O.' he did have moments when his behaviour did not really merit this description! The first time I ever took him to the vet's, before any vet had so much as touched him, he decided that he had no wish to be anywhere near a vet, and made this quite clear! He would suddenly seem to change character, and my loving, well behaved, happy dog, would disappear. His tail would go down, he would be uncooperative, and ignore any attempts staff made to befriend him, and at times his lips would draw back in a threatening manner, although he never snarled or attempted to go for anyone. He didn't appear to be afraid, although I expect he was, just determined to have nothing to do with them.

He was a definite sort of dog, and it was hard to change his mind once he had formed an opinion on anything. It did not matter how many treats vets gave him, or how friendly they were, it cut no ice with Jesse. He ate the treats, and then simply refused to let them get near him. Although he rarely had need of the vet before his final illnesses, he did occasionally pull a muscle, and need routine injections, so this was something of a problem. The vets suggested I should put a muzzle on him, which I did, but he had it off within 30 seconds, so it wasn't much help! I decided to take him to the vet's every week, over quite a long period, and we would wander round the waiting room and then I would give him a treat, and make a great fuss of him, in the hope that he would see the vet's as a less hostile place, but to no avail. He was bright enough to realise that the waiting room was fine, and he was quite happy to go into it, but the vet's room was another story, and that's when the trouble began!

He was also very suspicious of the scales at the vet's, and flatly refused to go near them, let alone on them. After weeks if not months of patient persuasion from me, he eventually consented to go onto them, but only if I went on as well, so we had to weigh both of us, then me alone and work out the difference to monitor his weight! An amused group of people in the waiting room would listen to me calling out my weight and our combined weights and the receptionist and me working out the difference between them!

Thinking about our problems at the vet's one day, I had an inspiration! I enjoy watching horse racing, and have noted that putting a hood over a horse's head will encourage it to allow itself to be led into the starting stalls, if it is reluctant to go. Would it work better for Jesse if he couldn't see what was going on? I considered it worth a try, so the next time we had cause to visit the vet I took a towel with me. Jesse liked towels and the whole process of being rubbed dry, so it had positive connotations.

I asked to see the most sympathetic of the vets at the practice, and explained my theory. He was happy to give it a go, as it would benefit him as well as us if Jesse was less difficult. We tried it out and it worked incredibly well; in fact he said afterwards that he would use the technique with other reluctant dogs. It worked like this: Jesse lay on his side on the floor, and I wrapped the towel loosely over his head, and knelt by him, encouraging and praising him all the time, whilst keeping the towel firmly in place. Although we could all hear the rumble of a growl on many occasions, he did lie still and consent to the vet touching him, injecting him, or manipulating his limbs as necessary, and this was a massive improvement.

It amazes me that more dogs are not like Jesse, since a trip to the vet's usually means some kind of pain or discomfort, but the vet explained to me that in his view Jesse was:

"....one of those highly intelligent, highly neurotic collies," and he fully understood the score, whereas many dogs can be 'bought off' with treats!

It was with a mixture of amusement, amazement and shame that I read on his file, written in red, that he was a very difficult dog, and warning all vets to be very careful of him. Jesse might have disliked being at the vets, but he would never had bitten anyone. He was just anxious and defensive, but, as always, OK if I was with him to reassure him. I felt I had to explain that he was a different dog outside of the vet's, but could see from their faces that they struggled to believe me!

Unfortunately I sometimes had to see vets who dismissed what I told them about handling Jesse, and one particularly unpleasant episode occurred in which a locum vet completely ignored my explanation about the towel method, and just told me to lift Jesse onto the table, which was designed for a small to medium sized dog. When I pointed this out, adding that it was therefore not big enough for a dog of Jesse's size, and also that I was unable to lift Jesse, as he was too heavy, he insisted we used the table, and said we would lift him together, him the back, and me the front. Without warning, he suddenly grabbed Jesse, and shoved him up onto the table, causing him to slide along it, bang his head on the wall, and find his legs disappearing from underneath him. I removed his head from the wall, set him on his legs again, and made my feelings clear to the vet, who commented that I had been of no help. He then told me that there was nothing wrong with Jesse (who, it seems, had pulled a muscle in one of his chasing expeditions) that couldn't be put right with rest and short lead walks for the next few weeks, and added:

"Of course, you people will insist on walking your dog miles, and you never take any notice of what I say, so I don't know why I bother."

I was absolutely furious, removed Jesse from the table with the help of a sympathetic nurse, and stormed out, telling him there was no way I was going to pay anything for such appalling treatment and that I would never bring my dog to see him again, and would warn others about him. I sent a letter of complaint to the head of the practice, who agreed that from then on I would only see him. This was a very positive step, as he was very calm, and 'laid back' and more than happy to take his time with Jesse and allow me to use the towel method to help Jesse to cope. In the last two years of his life, Jesse and I saw a great deal of this vet, who was unfailingly calm, supportive and optimistic. Jesse was eventually pretty good about seeing him, and he helped us both tremendously, not only through his expertise, but by the kind and understanding and positive way he treated us.

Mutual love and support for each other

As the years went by, Jesse continued to be a very active dog, and we became closer and closer all the time. We were very rarely apart, and always delighted to be re-united after a short separation. For some of his life, I was living alone, but it never felt like that, because Jesse was always there, looking out for me, loving me, protecting me, up for anything, and accompanying me everywhere I went. He also kept me pretty fit, as we walked for at least 2 hours every day. If we had the time and the inclination, we would sometimes walk on the moors or up and down the cliff path for anything up to 3 hours, and, as my left leg got stronger and stronger, it eventually recovered its full function and I had no more pain and swelling. I sometimes thought back to those awful dark months in hospital, which I had spent lying in bed, in constant pain, unable to do hardly anything for myself, (including showering or getting to the bathroom) and never breathing in fresh air, let alone seeing a blade of grass. Even after I was discharged I had a very arduous two years, when I had to use a wheelchair and then slowly progress to staggering around on crutches, wondering what on earth the future might hold. And now, here I was, albeit 15 years later, striding across the moors, totally independent and free, enjoying the wonders of nature, and inhaling the sweet country air, with this beautiful dog at my side. This really was a remarkable achievement, and a totally unexpected one, considering the gloomy prognosis I had been given, and I am quite sure that if I had not had Jesse to motivate me it would never have happened.

The aftermath of the car accident was not entirely physical, unfortunately, and I undoubtedly suffered from undiagnosed Post Traumatic Stress, which was less well understood in those days. I had been the passenger in the car, which had been in a head on collision with another car. I could see that this collision was imminent, and done everything I could to alert the driver to this, but unfortunately he appeared to be unable to swerve to avoid the collision. This was very probably because he had had too much to drink, despite my frantic efforts to dissuade him during the evening which preceded the accident. I had seriously contemplated not getting into the car with him, since he insisted on driving whatever I said, but I was in a foreign country, with no money, and we were 10 miles away from the place where we were staying, so I felt I had little choice. I would have driven myself, but had left my licence at home as he knew the country we were visiting and I did not, so it had seemed sensible for him to drive. Despite his intake of alcohol, he was not slurring his words, or staggering or showing any signs of being drunk, so having got in the car with him I had hoped for the best. Sadly, the best did not happen. He drove on the wrong side of the road, and despite my efforts to get him to move over, including screaming at him, he had continued to drive straight into an oncoming car. Perhaps I should have grabbed the steeling wheel, but my reactions were too slow. He was driving a Fiat Panda, the cheapest of the rental cars and in those days very poor on safety (again, despite my efforts to persuade him to upgrade to a safer car at the beginning of the holiday) and fortunately for the other people they were driving a Volvo Estate, and had slowed right down anticipating what might happen.

I remained conscious throughout the collision and the aftermath, which was very frightening, as the car we were in had been very badly damaged, as a result of which I became trapped in it by my left leg. The driver was even more badly injured than I was and was unconscious. The people in the other car, sustained only minor injuries and tried to pull me out of the car, as they were afraid it might explode as petrol was leaking everywhere They smashed the windscreen and dragged me out, probably damaging my leg further, although for the best of intentions, whilst the driver, although unconscious kept up a loud screaming. He was taken off by ambulance relatively quickly, but I was left at the roadside while another ambulance was called to take me to a different hospital. The country we were staying in was quite remote, and the health facilities were somewhat basic, compared to the ones we have here in the UK. For example, the operating theatre was filthy, and there was no nursing care. I was very fortunate that my daughter flew over to take care of me. She saw the car, and said it was like a concertina, and she couldn't believe anyone could have got out of it alive! The driver was in Intensive Care for two weeks but in the end survived and we were flown home, but he sustained brain damage, had a complete personality change and became very violent. After we were discharged, we were living together, as we were in a relationship, but his violence towards me was such that I had to get out very quickly one night, and ended up homeless and penniless as well as badly injured.

The trauma this involved stayed with me, and I had a lot of flashbacks and nightmares as well as an ongoing low level fear that something awful was going to happen again. I understand that this is not uncommon in post traumatic stress.

Jesse had this enviable way of living in the moment, as most animals do. He was not troubled by past events or worries about the future, but just lived each day as it came and fully appreciated everything that went on around him. Learning from him to see life in this way helped me to focus on the present, and let go of thoughts of the past, and gradually the nightmares diminished and the constant level of fear receded, as I always felt cherished and protected by Jesse. The flashbacks became fewer, as I found myself more and more able to live in the moment and embrace the present, banishing the past to where it belonged. To be able to live fully in the moment, and be actively aware of everything around you is part of what I believe is now called Mindfulness, which has become quite popular. It certainly has its advantages, as thinking about past traumas, or worrying about future possibilities can often be a poor and even destructive use of time. I certainly found that as time went by, living in the moment with Jesse by my side and enjoying watching his activities gave me less time for brooding, and reliving the past, and was extremely helpful in moving forward emotionally. Cognitive Behavioural therapy is often used to help people with PTSD, and involves replacing one thought with another, more constructive one, so that gradually unhelpful thought patterns are replaced by more positive ones. This happened to me because of living with Jesse. If flashbacks occurred, or I felt an overwhelming fear coming into my mind, I could reduce the impact of them by focussing on what Jesse and I were doing together, replacing dark thoughts with plans for the next walk, or an expedition of some kind which we would both enjoy. If I woke from a nightmare, I could always turn to Jesse for comfort, and he would always seem to know how I was feeling and calm my fears, just by his reassuring presence and love. Having Jesse gave me a positive and happy present and a daily purpose in life which slowly eclipsed the horrors of the past.

During the eleven and a half years of his life, my life was quite unsettled at times, with two relationship break-ups and house moves. Sometimes I became very upset, and would hide myself away to cry so as not to upset him, but he always found me, and comforted me by licking my face and rolling over next to me. Other times I would just hold him and cry into his beautiful soft hairy coat, and again, he would lick me and comfort me.

We would delight in each others' company, and just enjoy being together, whether on walks, in the house, with friends, at choir practice, or at work. He was a hugely important part of my life, and always wanted to be with me, whatever I was doing. We knew each other so well, that I rarely had to worry whether he would be OK in any situation. I just knew that if he was with me, we could face more or less anything together. He taught me so much, just by being who he was, a dog who was full of enthusiasm, love of life and happy to live in the moment and make the best of everything that he encountered.

He always did exactly as he liked on walks, as he knew the expectations I had of him, so I never really had to call him, or interfere with his activities in any way, and I took the view that walks were his time, and I would accommodate his interests, running, sniffing, playing with other dogs, playing ball, chasing things, whatever he wanted, really, he did. We both enjoyed walking, and got bored easily, so walks were very varied as well as long, and always a wonderful time of being together. I had realised, by the time he was about two years old, that he would always want to shoot off, chasing things, racing around with other dogs, exploring or just running for the joy of it, and that I had no need to try to restrict his activities or keep him in sight. He was just doing his own thing and would always return, and always know exactly where I was.

Another activity we shared was rather more unusual...shopping! Jesse was the only male I have ever met who did not get impatient or bored during a shopping expedition. I could not take him into supermarkets, of course, but apart from that, we used to do a lot of shopping together. He was a great favourite at the greengrocers, where he queued up for a dog biscuit from the kind owners of the shop; he also loved the pet shop, and would always walk purposefully towards it as we passed, and look very disappointed if I told him we weren't going into it that day. He was allowed into one of the butchers, and although he found it hard to restrain himself with all that tasty meat on display, he always managed it.

He was surprisingly good when I was shopping for clothes and shoes. In the shoe shop he would wait patiently while I browsed and then tried on lots of pairs of shoes, walking up and down with me as I tried them out. I only went into clothes shops which allowed dogs to go in, and this worked quite well, as my preference was for casual country style clothes shops, and charity shops, most of which were dog friendly. When I went into the changing room, Jesse would come with me with reluctance, as he didn't like the confined space. If it was a room with a curtain, he insisted on standing with his head sticking out under the curtain, hence amusing other shoppers, and exposing me to embarrassment if he pulled the curtain up too far! But he seemed to enjoy these expeditions, and I would not have wanted to go without him, even though he never commented on whether or not he approved of my purchases!

As I have mentioned, Jesse was a one woman dog, and would always bark if a friend tried to give me a hug in greeting or parting. I was never sure whether he was protecting me or whether perhaps he was a bit jealous, or maybe some of each. He barked at anyone who came to the door or into the church when I was practising on my own, and had a very loud deep bark, which was quite scary. He never followed it up by snarling or looking as if he might attack anyone, but I suppose it was his way of letting them know he was there to protect me.

A new experience for Jesse was travelling by bus. The first time we went on a bus together, I had left my car in the garage for a service. I decided to get the bus back home, as the walk back was along the main road, and I didn't want Jesse breathing in traffic fumes. I was slightly surprised to be asked to pay for him. The driver explained the system:

"His ticket is called a 'Dog Rover'. With that he can travel all day on any bus he likes in the county, so it is well worth the money, a real bargain!"

In my imagination, I had wonderful visions of Jesse deciding to have a day out using his Dog Rover ticket. He would probably head for the moors and run for miles before catching the bus home. Or maybe he would catch several busses to go to different parts of the county on his day out. He would then return, tired, but proud of his independence and happy from his day out, just pleasing himself and going where he chose! I felt it was inappropriate to share this vision with the driver, as he would think I was quite mad, but it amused me all the way home, and has continued to amuse me from time to time!

However, in reality, I think he would have chosen to give the busses a miss. I had cause to take him on the bus several times, but he was not at all keen to go. He would wait by my side quietly and not cause a fuss, but wore a pained expression on his face, and was always delighted to get off again.

As for trains, he really hated them, both inside and out! A friend once persuaded me to go for a walk which involved getting the train back home. Jesse was most reluctant to get on, and once inside just stood shaking all over, as near the door as possible. This was the first and last time I took him on a train. He hated the noise and fumes and smell, and the fact that it was crowded. He was also frightened of trains when they went past us when we were out and about; the noise and impact of a train going past him was anathema to Jesse , and we did our best to avoid them.

Although many people would disagree, I feel that having a dog is really a way of life. I am not saying that you can't have a dog and a job and a family and integrate them all in such a way that the dog can lead a happy and purposeful life, but when I look back on my life with Jesse, I think we gained so much from each other's company because we moulded our lives around each other. I did not engage in activities which meant leaving Jesse alone for long periods. I could have spent time swimming, going to lots of concerts, joining several choirs, joining other groups such as Pilates or poetry reading, all of which I have an interest in, but they would have meant leaving Jesse on his own. I could have gone on foreign holidays and left him with a dog minder, but I would not have wanted to, because I would have missed him too much.

Jesse and I developed a life style which meant we could both be happy doing things together, and that involved compromise on both sides: Jesse adapting to spending long hours in churches while I practised the organ, and to being quiet and still at meetings and during choir practises, and me reciprocating by taking him on walks in places I knew he would enjoy and avoiding walking in places I knew he would have found boring, (along lanes or cycle paths for example). And so, over the years I began to realise that compromise doesn't just mean giving up things for someone else, it can open the door to a very close, meaningful and rewarding relationship. For someone as independent as I am, that was a useful insight, and has made me a more considerate person, I hope.

New Zealand

I had a phone call from my sister's husband in New Zealand. This was very unusual, and could only mean one thing: trouble. He told me that she had been ill for many months but had been reluctant to go and see a doctor until things got so bad she couldn't stand it anymore. She had never mentioned this to me. The diagnosis was cancer and she had totally freaked out. Could I come and help her through this?

This posed a huge problem for me, although clearly nothing like as huge a problem as my sister was facing. Since the car accident I had developed a phobia about flying, and I had tried but failed to get on board a plane as part of a course for people such as me, so I wasn't confident I would be able to do it. Naturally I wanted to help but what if I couldn't manage the flight? Just as great a concern was what would happen to Jesse? On the other hand, how could I just refuse and leave her to face this terrible situation with no family around her, and not many friends, as she is quite a reserved person, who does not make friends easily. I knew her husband, although caring and well-meaning, would have difficulty in giving her the kind of emotional support she needed. I struggled to decide how I could sort myself and Jesse out so that I could go and help her. I thought of Jesse and his stalwart love for me. He would have done anything to help me, and I him. Surely I could overcome the difficulties and give her the same sort of love that Jesse gave me?

I didn't know how either Jesse or I would cope with a separation of more than a few hours, as we had bonded so closely, and Jesse struggled to spend time with other people and without me, even though he managed it when I went to see my children and grandchildren. That was a bit different, though, because it was usually only for 24 hours or so. After much thought I decided I must go to New Zealand, and asked if I could leave Jesse with a friend who was a registered dog fosterer, and whom Jesse knew very well. He would also be able to see other friends of mine, whom he knew well and lived nearby, and who agreed to take him on walks with their dogs, so it was probably the best situation I could find for him while I was away, although I knew he would struggle with it.

I did manage to get on the plane and get through the journey, with a break, without passing out or being sick or any of the other things which had happened to me before when I had tried to fly. Maybe the urgency of the situation saw me through, but in any event I managed it and eventually arrived in New Zealand.

Although it was lovely to see my sister and her husband, the circumstances were far from ideal, and I spent a great deal of time trying to comfort her and maintain an optimistic stance, as well as giving practical help. However, she was truly freaked out by her diagnosis, especially since there has never been anyone in our family who has had cancer, and it never crossed either of our minds that we might get it. I don't know how typical her reaction to the diagnosis was, or if, in fact there is any 'typical' reaction. Maybe everyone feels differently and reactions vary. In any event, her emotions were very mixed; at times she would be very depressed and say it wasn't worth going through all that treatment just to die anyway; at other times she would be angry, and rail at the unfairness of it; sometimes she would simply deny that the diagnosis was correct, thinking about all the things she still wanted to do with her life, and looking forward to a future she had taken for granted. At yet other times she would try to be calm and positive, knowing that it is very important with cancer to maintain a positive attitude and reduce stress as far as possible. Happy to try complimentary medicine, she spent a lot of time and money on this form of treatment, and also on finding out the best foods to eat, but it is hard to say how much it helped. I tried to encourage her to do ordinary things and take her mind off thinking about cancer, but it was not easy, of course.

Her predominant feeling was that she didn't want to engage with the medical profession and go through the whole process of further diagnosis, treatment, prognosis and all that this would entail. Her husband and I were naturally worried about this, as we felt it was essential that she did, if there was to be any chance of recovery. She particularly disliked the Oncologist who had not only told her she had cancer in an insensitive way, but also been very negative about her prognosis. When the time came for her to go to her next appointment with him, she couldn't face it. I knew the appointment had to be kept, so she could be on track for treatment, so the only solution I could come up with was for me to go instead! This is not quite as silly as it sounds, as we are close in age and look very similar. Fortunately it was an appointment to discuss results and future treatment, rather than one which involved practical tests. I went to see him, and he was indeed very negative about the prognosis, drawing me a diagram which showed that within a year 70% of patients with this particular form of cancer would be dead. The other 30% would die within 5 years. We went on to discuss treatment, and it was only at the end of the appointment that he looked at me very closely and inquired:

"Are you sure you're my patient? You look a bit different from last time I saw you!"

I had to come clean and tactfully explain the situation, but I had the information I needed, did not tell my sister about the graph, gave her a positive report of the consultation, and kept her on track for the treatment she so badly needed. It took a lot of persuasion to get her to the hospital for an appointment with another Oncologist who is a specialist in the type of cancer she had, but this time we were successful and she found this Oncologist to be much more approachable, positive and optimistic than the previous one, and consented to undergo the treatment she so desperately needed.

Amongst all the tears and panic and shock, there were good times, though. New Zealand is such a beautiful place, outside the cities, and I had visited it regularly for some years because of family connections, and always enjoyed the deserted beaches, acres of unspoiled land and wonderful sense of space which New Zealand offers. We had lovely walks with their dogs, and I took the younger one daily on a trail through the bush, which offered exotic bushes, trees and birds, and breathtaking views. My sister had a piano, and I played and we sang together, and it was good that she felt able to talk to me about her feelings and fears, and I was there to listen and try to provide positive thoughts and suggestions, and to give her strength and hope. Her husband was supportive and we worked well together as a team.

But those three weeks were awful, in terms of being separated from Jesse. I missed him all the time, and really felt as if part of me was missing. Every night I would go through the photos I had of him on my mobile phone, and try to communicate with him across the miles, by focussing my thoughts and mind entirely on him, and sending him non-verbal messages of love and comfort. I didn't know what he was thinking, or feeling, but was afraid he would think I had abandoned him, or didn't love him anymore, and maybe he would think he would never see me again. I know dogs are much more sensitive than we are to non verbal senses, and have remarked on this earlier, and I really hoped that by focussing my mind as strongly as I could on him, he might receive some kind of awareness of my thoughts, giving him comfort and reassurance. It was the only thing I could do.

I knew he trusted me, and I could only hope that he had faith that I would return as soon as possible, but how can a dog know these things, when they are suddenly left with someone else? I knew he would miss me terribly, although I knew he would be well looked after physically, and given lots of affection, and despite receiving reassuring messages from my friend that he was eating and enjoying his walks, I felt totally cut off from him, and worried about him all the time.

I left my sister much better than when I had arrived, well on the way to undergoing a treatment programme, and eventually she recovered and at this time, several years later, is completely free of cancer.

The journey home from New Zealand seemed to take forever, and I became increasingly excited as it neared its end. When I eventually arrived at my friend's house, Jesse went absolutely mad, racing round and round, hurling himself on me, his tail wagging so much that he nearly took off! I just sat and hugged him and felt tears of joy and relief pouring down my face. Never had it felt so good to see him and hold him again. He had put on a bit of weight, as she had misunderstood my feeding instructions, and let him eat ad lib. Maybe he had also aged a little, perhaps he had been as worried about me as I had about him, or maybe he really had thought I had abandoned him, but none of it mattered any more. All that mattered was that we were together, and I determined that we would never be parted like that again. Afterwards he always greeted the friend who had looked after him with enthusiasm, so I felt reassured that he must have enjoyed at least in some degree the time he had spent with her!

I heard a programme on the radio the other day, in which a man was talking about his love for his father. He said that he thought that to love someone is to try to see everything they are and to love them for it, in all their complexity. I agree so much with his thoughts, and it was so true for Jesse and me. We were neither of us perfect, but we knew each other, loved each other and accepted each other for exactly who we were. Never in my life had I had a relationship with anyone where I fully accepted and appreciated them exactly as they were, and vice versa, apart from my children, when they were little, but Jesse taught me how to do this, and how wonderful it is to love and be loved in such a way.

Jesse's illness

One day, as he was barking at the postman, I heard Jesse gasp for breath. This didn't seem right, so, thinking he had a cold, I took him to the vet, but she thought he might have heart problems. I was extremely worried, but on further investigation, it turned out not to be his heart but his larynx. He had paralysis of the larynx. I insisted that he should be referred to the best veterinary hospital in the area, as there was talk of an operation, and I wanted him to be in the best possible hands, and there the diagnosis was confirmed. Worse, I was told it was caused by an underlying neuropathy, which was already detectable in his hind legs via their diagnostic machine. They said that within three to six months, his breathing would become so bad he would only be able to walk 100 metres before collapsing. At that point, they would have to do a 'tie back' operation, in which the vocal chords were tied back so they couldn't obstruct his breathing. This would bring problems such as an increased risk of infection, and make swimming impossible, but would enable him to continue with his life relatively normally. The neuropathy might advance slowly or quickly, but was progressive and would weaken his muscles, eventually making his hind legs dysfunctional.

I could not believe any of this. Jesse was so fit and well, and had always run miles without any difficulty in breathing and his hind legs were so strong that he still jumped over gates and groins on the beach with ease.

I could only think it was an incorrect-diagnosis, and that it must be some kind of some kind of cold virus and would soon get better. He was only 9 years old, and Collies are usually quite long lived...he was only just over half way through his natural life span.

And then, as if this diagnosis wasn't appalling enough, a couple of weeks later a friend of mine felt a small lump under his chin. I could feel it too, and thought it might be to do with loose vocal chords, but I took him to the vet anyway for a check. They sent us straight back to the referral hospital.

There they confirmed that it was not just vocal chords flopping around, but almost certainly a form of cancer. The surgeon thought it might be cancer of the thyroid, and if so, it was very early stage, and he had a good chance of removing it, which would have resulted in a complete cure, with a bit of luck. But when he operated, he discovered that it was a very rare soft tissue cancer, and there was no way of removing it because of the blood vessels around it. If he had tried to cut it out, Jesse would have bled to death on the operating table. I was directed to see the Oncologist, who informed me starkly that this type of soft tissue cancer was very rare and very aggressive, and he only had a few weeks to live. There was an experimental treatment programme we could put him on, but no statistical evidence that it would make any difference. She had only seen 4 dogs with this condition, and they had all died within weeks. According to the veterinary text books, this was the norm.

It is impossible to describe the devastation I felt, and I was fortunate to have my daughter and a friend with me for support. I drove home in a complete daze that day; I have no idea how I got through the following days and weeks of shock, grief and disbelief. I could not accept what they were telling me, I knew it had to be a mistake; it could not possibly be true. He was a relatively young dog, still full of life, and should have had several happy years ahead of him. He didn't seem ill and was still full of energy. And yet they were both highly regarded experts. The Oncologist's words went round and round in my head, but didn't make any sense. Then there was the neuropathy diagnosis. If Jesse couldn't breathe because of the paralysis of the larynx, and they couldn't do the tie back operation because the cancer was in his throat, in the way, then what? I couldn't bear to think about it. Every morning I woke up thinking it could not be true, maybe it was just a nightmare, maybe things would be OK after all, and then slowly realised that in all probability it was true, it had happened, he really was seriously ill and likely to die. Such things didn't happen to us, they couldn't happen to us, they happened to other people you read about or saw on TV, but not to people like us who were so happy together and who had expected years of happiness to lie ahead. I could not conceive of life without Jesse, he was by now an integral part of me. Anyway Jesse appeared to be perfectly alright apart from his bark, which had diminished in volume and was higher in pitch.

Unfortunately, but predictably, we had had the usual problems at the Veterinary Hospital, because the surgeon was very opposed to giving Jesse a sedative before he took him through to anesthetise and operate on him. I explained that if he just took Jesse through without me, Jesse would fight tooth and nail, as he would think a stranger was taking him away from me, and that it would be better to sedate him in the waiting room, where I could be with him, and comfort him until he was too dozy to know what was going on. Alternatively, would I be allowed to go through with him? The surgeon took the former option, with much complaint, ("it's not our practice here...") but I was amused this time to note that again there was red writing all over Jesse's file! Even though he was sedated, he had clearly not appreciated the attentions of this particular vet.

In sharp contrast, Jesse took a great liking to the Oncologist, and was never any trouble at all when she examined him. We didn't even need to use the towel!

When I watch programmes such as 'Supervet' on TV, it never fails to amaze me that dogs happily trot through to the treatment area, their leads held by complete strangers, and co-operate with unfamiliar vets and nurses. Was Jesse really the only one who objected to this? I find it hard to believe. I also feel that it is sad that when a beloved pet most needs you, i.e. when they are feeling unwell and vulnerable, you are expected to just hand them over, like an object, and not allowed to be there to comfort and reassure them. No doubt there are hygiene and other reasons for this, but I always felt I let Jesse down by not being there for him on these occasions, and absolutely hated having to leave him overnight after he had undergone an operation.

All the usual questions went through my mind. Why Jesse? What had he ever done but be a wonderful loving loyal dog? Was it genetic? Was it anything I had done? I had given him the best possible food, loads of exercise, lots of love, minimal stress, kept him away from traffic fumes, looked after him as best I could. Why should he have to go through all this, with the likelihood of dying years before his natural lifespan would have ended? What had caused it?

These questions remain with me, but I have found no answers

Our fight against Jesse's illnesses

Despite these terrible prognoses, Jesse did not in fact die within a few weeks, or a few months, come to that. He far outlived his prognoses and made medical history while he was about it! I think there were a variety of reasons for this, but I think the greatest was love. I will try to explain. I decided that I was not going to give up without a fight, and I was not going to accept the inevitability that Jesse would die an early death. After all, the cancer was apparently so rare that the Oncologist had only ever seen four dogs with the same condition, and very little was known about it, so how could they be sure of the prognosis? I have had some dire prognoses myself, over the years, which have turned out to be much exaggerated, and have learned the value of self help and a positive attitude. Jesse had helped me so much to overcome my health issues, and I was determined to repay this by helping him as much as I could in return.

I knew that Jesse, like me, would fight all the way against ill health, as he had such a strong life force, and such a love of life. It was one of things that had attracted me to him as a puppy, when I first set eyes on him. He was so full of life, initiating games, pushing to the front for food, annoying the older dogs, always rushing around. I thought of him swimming for his life against a ferocious tide when he got stuck on a sandbank on that traumatic day, and I knew that Jesse would be a more than willing partner in the fight I proposed to put up!

With my agreement, the Oncologist put Jesse on the experimental treatment, and I rang the hospital to inquire whether they had a dog nutritionist there, which they didn't. I found one via the Internet who sounded competent and committed, and enlisted her help. She formulated a diet for him, and advised a number of supplements which would maximise the value he got from his food and help his immune system. The diet involved a lot of cooking, and was based on sweet potato, swede, turnip, an apple and a small quantity of broccoli and blueberries, with chicken, liver and oily fish for protein. Throughout his illness, she was a fantastic guide and support to us both.

Jesse loved his new diet, and ate heartily, but he did not love going to see the physiotherapist to whom he was referred for the neuropathy, (which they assured me was real, even if there were currently no signs of it except for his breathing difficulties). She was a lovely, gentle, kind person, but his prescribed treatment was to walk on a machine filled with water up to the top of his legs (like the walking/running machines you get in human gyms, but with water added and enclosed sides to retain it). The idea was that this would strengthen his muscles as he walked against the water pressure. Unfortunately, it was very narrow, especially for a big dog like Jesse, and he could only just fit into it without touching the sides. He went into it, after much encouragement, but when she turned it on and he had to walk inside it, he hated it, and kept up a continuous stream of 'crying'. I think he just hated being trapped inside the machine, and not being in control of what was happening to him. He had always hated any sort of confinement, and appeared quite unable to cope. However much I tried to encourage him, from outside the machine, it made no difference. He might have been better if I had been walking in there with him, but that was not allowed. When the physiotherapist wanted to massage and manipulate his muscles, he refused to let her get anywhere near him, but just ran around the room avoiding her, as he associated her with the machine.

We persisted for a while, but he never got used to it, and became worse, not better, and during the third session, I just cried with him, as I couldn't bear to see him so distressed. The physiotherapist stopped the walking machine.

"We can't go on like this," she said, kindly but sadly. "It's doing him more harm than good, and the stress is really bad for you both".

"I'm sorry", I snuffled."I know you are doing everything you can to help, but he just can't cope, and I can't bear to see him so distressed, when he already has so much to cope with. Is there not something similar he and I can do together which he can tolerate? "

There was a possibility that I could have taken him to a local therapy pool, to strengthen his muscles by swimming, which he would have enjoyed, but they refused to let me go in with him, I don't know why, and I knew he would not tolerate going in with strangers.

Wisely, she gave me an exercise sheet and advised us to do as much physiotherapy as we could at home, which we did very diligently! This involved me massaging his muscles, which he loved, and us both walking up as many hills as we could find to strengthen his back legs. We also walked up and down the stairs in the house several times a day. Instead of the water therapy, I encouraged him to swim as much as possible, either in the sea or in rivers.

Jesse's amazing zest for life, which helped him to far outlive his prognoses

Life continued with lots of walks and playing with sticks and balls and toys, and as much swimming as possible, and the 'few weeks' he was supposed to have left to live, were soon behind us. Jesse appeared to be fine. We did our exercises, and lots of uphill walking to strengthen his legs, and he continued to play with other dogs and show his customary zest for life. His breathing did not cause him a problem most of the time, even when he was dashing around, although occasionally he ran out of breath for a few moments and had to rest until it came back. There was certainly no sign of him flaking out after walking for a few hundred metres as the original vet had suggested he would, so he never needed the tie back operation which he wouldn't have been able to have anyway. He had to go for blood and urine tests every month, but on the whole they were acceptable. Oddly, Jesse refused to drink water shortly after he was diagnosed with cancer, so it had to be chicken or vegetable broth. Unfortunately, he enjoyed the taste so much that he was constantly demanding a drink, and when I realised how much he was drinking, I had to start rationing it, as it was just washing away a lot of the nutrients in his food.

We had a scare once when his kidneys seemed to be suffering from the effects of the medication, but an adjustment in his diet sorted this out.

Every night we had a ritual, when I would brush his teeth, and say some prayers, and I think we both derived strength and comfort from this. It always ended with me saying:

"I love you Jesse, and I always will. I will always be with you, never leave you, and whatever the future holds, we will face it together, always and forever."

A year went by, and Jesse was still functioning pretty much as normal. It would have been hard to tell that there was anything wrong with him. He had gained a few more grey hairs, and slowed down a little, but we still walked for an hour and a half a day, divided into two or three walks, and he still had an excellent quality of life, and came everywhere with me. He showed no sign of pain, and his bark came back loud and strong. One of the worries when a dog (or human) is taking chemotherapy is sickness and diarrhoea. Jesse avoided this, probably because the nutritionist put him on supplements to guard against it, and it was never a problem. Also, most cancer patients lose weight, but again, thanks to the nutritionist, Jesse never did.

However, we had one occasion when he was sick, just the one, and I am quite sure it was not the chemo that caused it.

I had been playing the organ in the local church for about 18 months, and everything was fine. Jesse always came with me. At first the choir master, who was in situ before I was appointed as the organist, was fine, but then he gradually became more and more negative towards me. I am not sure why, but he was very 'old school' and it may he been that he disliked having to work with a female organist who knew a lot more about music than he did! I tried to be tactful and positive towards him but it wasn't really working out. Things came to a head during Jesse's illness, and so I agreed to meet with him and the Vicar to try to sort things out. Sadly the choir master used the occasion not to try to resolve matters, but to heap more abuse on my head, and said some very cruel things, as the Vicar looked at the floor and seemed unable to handle the situation. I tried to make some constructive suggestions as to a way forward, but the men made no comment on these. We were getting nowhere and I was feeling very much under attack and very upset. Suddenly Jesse was sick, very sick, all over the carpet. As the men fussed around, ineffectually dabbing at it with kitchen roll, I informed them that my dog was far more important than petty squabbles which should never have happened in the first place, suggested they sort out the music situation themselves and that my first priority was my dog. I would return later to clear up the mess with the proper equipment and substances. Jesse and I swept out and I gave him a drink and took him to the vet, but there was no physical cause, as far as we could see. My opinion is that he just couldn't take listening to this horrible and unmerited attack on the person he loved so much and it made him physically sick. He was never sick again.

Perhaps inevitably, but incredibly sadly, as time went on, Jesse gradually became weaker and found it increasingly difficult to play with other dogs, and to do more than his 'collie lope' on a walk. We still played ball, but I used to bounce or throw or roll it to him, as he couldn't really chase it any more. He tried to pick up sticks, but quickly dropped them again. I think they pressed on the cancer, which was slowly and ominously growing around his throat, and no doubt spreading round his body. He developed a limp in his right front leg, which the vet and I thought might be arthritis. I gave him two types of pills for this and it got better, but then his eyes started clouding over. The vet said his eyesight, although impaired, was still functional, and so it proved to be, but it must have been an additional burden for Jesse to bear.

As Jesse's health slowly deteriorated, I had a friend who helped me in two ways: one practical and one emotional. Firstly, he suggested that a poem he knew might help to give me strength and courage. Although it was about war, and keeping faith and strength in the face of adversity in battle, it made sense to me, since this was indeed a series of battles in the war against both cancer and neuropathy. I learnt the poem by heart, and used to say it frequently to Jesse, and I believe it gave us both some strength and determination while we were fighting our battle against his illnesses. The poem is called:

Say not the Struggle nought availeth: by Arthur Hugh Clough

The other help he gave me was practical. He suggested he might come and be in my house with Jesse if I ever had to go out without him, as I did not want to leave Jesse at all, both in case he had breathing difficulties and because he knew he was ill, and was afraid and anxious about being left alone. My friend honoured his word and although we did not need him for some time, when we did, he was always there for us, however inconvenient it was for him, and however risky, as looking after a sick dog is not an easy task, and not one which most people would have taken on. Jesse and I were both extremely grateful for his kindness.

One day Jesse and I were walking on the marshes, and I said to him:

"Do you remember how you used to chase the ducks here? You used to charge through dykes and over rough ground and bark, and follow, wagging your tail, until they were just specks in the sky! Oh Jesse, I would give anything to be able to watch you do that, just one last time!"

Shortly after I had spoken, he disappeared with a rustle of long grass, and there he was, chasing ducks and swimming after them in the dyke!

This was the last time he did anything like this, and I have no doubt in my mind that he understood what I said and made a huge effort to accommodate my wishes, at whatever cost to himself, which would have been considerable, I expect. I cannot believe it was a co-incidence, but it did make me happy for a while, to see some of the old spark was still there.

As he became more ill, people we met started asking whether he was old, which annoyed and upset me. My answer was always that he was not old, but ill, and doing his best to cope with two horrible conditions, which had aged us both. I wondered whether they asked people they met 'are you old?' when they started going grey and slowing down, or appeared to be unwell, and why they thought it was OK to make such comments about my dog who would always be beautiful in my eyes.

Jesse's courage in the face of adversity

Despite these signs that the illnesses were beginning to win the war, Jesse was a fighter. He loved life and he loved me and he didn't want to leave me and die. He was so brave and uncomplaining and I really admired his courage. He was an example to us all. He never whined, never complained, was always up for a walk or any kind of outing and always ate with enthusiasm, even when he was clearly not feeling too good. He began to get infections frequently, although they were usually sorted out with antibiotics, and was very up and down in his general health. It was an incredibly difficult time for me emotionally, as I kept thinking he was nearing the end, and then he would bounce back, and start being much more lively and energetic.

The summer was a problem for Jesse because he got very hot very quickly and this affected his breathing. The vet told me that every time he became hot and panted, the cancer swelled up in his throat, making his air passage even smaller. But we managed. We developed an unusual, but effective regime, which involved us walking at 7.00am and 11.00pm and keeping out of the heat in between. It made life tricky for me, but enabled him to survive through the summer. I also bought him a 'cool coat' which is a recent development in dog equipment. The coat is made of an absorbent material which you soak in cold water, wring out and then put on the dog. Slowly it absorbs the heat from the dog, and dries out, hence keeping the dog cooler in hot sunny days.

Eventually Jesse did start to have difficulty in breathing again, but we evolved a way of managing it. He would make a roaring noise, and collapse and roll over. I developed a technique whereby I got him to sit up and lean against me, and held his nose upwards, to increase the air flow, all the while stroking him, and talking to him calmly. I breathed slowly and deeply and it encouraged him to do the same, so we were breathing together. This seemed to help, and the attacks became fewer and shorter in duration, and, as summer turned to autumn, they eventually ceased altogether.

Unfortunately, during the period of time he was having these breathing difficulties, I needed to leave him for a few hours, which I really did not want to have to do. The friend I mentioned earlier was, for once, unable to help, so I asked some close friends, whom Jesse liked and trusted, whether they could look after him for me. They kindly agreed, even though it was a big responsibility. I asked them not to take Jesse out for a walk with their dogs, as I was not sure he would manage it, as they walked their dogs a long way. I was a bit worried about him being left alone, in case he had breathing difficulties, but my friend said it would not be a problem, as her husband would be at home for most of the day, and they would ensure someone was with him at all times. I explained the technique I used to help him to return to normal after one of these breathless attacks.

I rushed back as soon as I could to collect him, but when I got there, he was alone in the house, and it was all locked up. He started barking and howling when he saw me through the window, and I couldn't bear to see him upset. It was truly horrendous to see my beloved dog on the other side of a glass window, and know I couldn't get to him, and I was terrified that the stress of the barking and howling would set off a breathing attack, and there would be no-one with him to help him.

My friends' house had a large wrought iron gate, about 3 metres high, with spikes on the top, which led into the back garden, and I knew that in the back garden was a dog flap into the back of the house, which they had probably left unlocked for Jesse. I thought it was just possible I could squeeze through the dog flap if I could manage to scale the gate. With great difficulty, I climbed the gate and accessed the back garden. I then managed to wriggle through the dog flap without getting stuck, with Jesse cheering me on throughout! Re-united, we were happy to sit together on the floor and hug each other, and this is how my friend found us when she returned 5 minutes later! The look on her face was priceless, as she simply couldn't believe how I had managed to get into the house! It turned out that her husband had been called away just before she returned from her dog walk, and Jesse had only been on his own for a few minutes, so no damage was done, and we had a cup of tea and a good laugh about it.

Two years passed, and Jesse was regarded by the Oncologist as something of a medical miracle, especially when he went into her room and started nosing about in her cupboards, still curious and interested in life, and still relatively active. According to the text books he should have been dead a long time ago. She said it was a good thing he had never read them, and also that in the light of his survival this long, they would have to re-write them.

We also had a brief moment of fame when we were the subject of an article written by me and posted by the Nutritionist on line in the Huffington Post. She wanted people to know how love, good care and excellent nutrition could help in these so called hopeless cases, where a dog has been given a terminal diagnosis. She told me many people just gave up, on hearing such a diagnosis, and had their dogs put to sleep straight away, whereas they could have enjoyed a bit more good quality life. She found us something of an inspiration and wanted to share our story. She also posted the article on her website, where it remained for 2 years after Jesse's death.

The two years and three months which Jesse and I had together following his diagnoses were marred, not only by him slowing down, but also by a constant nagging anxiety in my mind. Was Jesse in pain? Was he going to slowly decline, or would the end come suddenly? What would happen at the end? How would I know when he had had enough, or would he just suffocate or choke to death one day? Worst of all, and never far away from my thoughts, was 'how will I ever live without him?'

I also had very positive moments, when I remembered to enjoy each day we had together and be grateful for the extra time we had, every day a bonus, considering the prognoses. We tried very hard to live each day to the full, one day at a time. Jesse was considerably more successful at this than I was!

I even began to believe at one stage that we might beat both these conditions, and enable him to live out his natural life span, but it turned out to be wishful thinking. In my more realistic moments, I was afraid that the illnesses would catch up with him eventually: it was just a case of which one killed him first.

During this period, I did wonder what might have happened if Jesse had not been neutered. Would I have asked someone to provide us with a bitch to have his puppies? If so, I could have had one, and Jesse could have lived on in him or her, as far as any individual can live on through their progeny. Would it have lessened the agony of parting with Jesse? I think it would, but it was not to be.

Although this period was full of anxiety and sadness, there were also moments of humour. After a year or so of allowing me to collect urine samples, Jesse decided that he wasn't going to do it anymore, and refused to let me get near him when he realised I was carrying the plastic bowl I used for the purpose. I would hide it behind my back, or under my coat, but he always knew when I had it and would shoot off way ahead of me to pee, ensuring I wouldn't be able to catch up with him. On the rare occasions I did, he would immediately put his leg down. One day I thought a frying pan might be better, as it had a wider base, and was walking up the road with it when a friend drove past. She stared in amazement.

"Whatever were you doing this morning with Jesse?" she asked when she saw me later that day.

"Was that really a frying pan in your hand?"

She laughed when I explained what I was trying to do, and we both wondered what the dog walkers in the area had made of it!

In desperation, I left him with a close 'doggy' friend for half an hour one day, and asked her if she could try to get a sample, as he would not suspect her, but when I came back, she reluctantly acknowledged defeat, despite her initial confidence that she would be able to do it. She had spent a considerable time chasing him round the garden, but to no avail!

As his health deteriorated, we had some terrifying experiences, which involved him being attacked by other dogs. It is well known that a pack of wolves, living naturally, will not always look after their sick or old members, especially if there is a shortage of food. Sick and old wolves slow the pack down, and are scented by predators, thereby becoming a danger to the whole pack. Because of this, it is not unusual for the younger stronger members to attack them.

I presume some of that instinct remains despite so many years of domestication of dogs today. As Jesse became less well, other dogs either ignored him, or showed signs of aggression towards him. This must have been really difficult for such a proud dog, who had always enjoyed playing with other dogs, and would never allow himself to be bullied when he was strong and healthy, but would retaliate with vigour.

The first incident occurred in the park. As we walked down the road towards it, I could hear a man shouting and screaming all the way round the park, obviously addressing his dogs. I began to walk towards the sound, although I couldn't see him, I don't know why, maybe with some vague notion of trying to dissuade him from treating his dogs that way. Anyway, when he came into view, he had stopped shouting and the dogs, two young Rottweilers, were walking to heel, looking subdued. I decided not to say anything, as generally speaking, in my experience, people think they know best about their dogs, and don't take kindly to any comments or take note of them, and in any event, the aggression he had been showing towards his dogs had stopped, at least for the moment. As we were going past them they suddenly attacked Jesse ferociously, without any warning. It was not just a case of noise and posturing, as you so often get with dogs, they were in deadly earnest. It was horrible to see, and very frightening, these two young dogs, working as a team, with deadly intent to destroy my beautiful dog. Their owner did nothing, but stood and watched. Jesse could not defend himself. He did not have the strength, but just stood looking scared and bewildered. So I weighed in, screamed at them, kicked them both in places which are most painful, hurled myself on them, and did everything I could to stop them. I managed to get them off him, and knelt down to see what damage they had done to Jesse. He was very shaken, as was I, but not seriously hurt, thank goodness. As I was doing this the owner began to shout abuse at me, for kicking his dogs, and claim that Jesse had initiated the fight. At this stage of his life, Jesse had gone very grey, especially around his face, and was clearly unsteady on his feet, looking older than he was.

"Really?" I said, in my most sarcastic voice. "A seriously ill dog suddenly decides to take on two young Rottweilers in the peak of health? How odd, I wonder why he should do that?"

His girlfriend, highly embarrassed, hustled him away, but I was so angry and upset at the way those dogs had gone for Jesse, and the man's prior treatment of them, which had probably triggered the aggression in the first place, that I would have continued the argument for as long as necessary, had he stayed, and said a great deal more than was wise. My opinion is that his dogs were so wound up by his shouting at them earlier that they felt the need to take their aggression out on someone or something, and unfortunately, it was Jesse. I was angry with myself for putting him at risk by walking towards them, and the whole episode brought home to me how ill he had become, causing other dogs to consider it OK to go for him like that, and him to realise he was quite unable to put up any fight against them.

The other incident was not dissimilar, and happened a few weeks later. We were walking in some deserted woods, and in the distance I heard a male voice calling for his dogs, calmly at first, and then increasingly urgently. Suddenly an Alsatian and a Doberman appeared out of the undergrowth. They circled Jesse, and starting snarling, as their owner continued to call them, but was too far away to take any action. Then they suddenly pounced. Again, Jesse was too ill to defend himself, and just cowered away. I was furious that they should do this to my beloved dog, and my anger gave me strength and courage.

"Don't you dare touch him!" I screamed at them at the top of my voice, looking directly into their eyes with real fury, (which you are not supposed to do, as they will apparently see this as a challenge and maybe turn their aggression on you as a result).

"Leave him alone. Get off him, both of you!"

I was past caring whether or not they would go for me, I just wanted them to leave Jesse alone.

I then stood as near them as I could get, and pointed in the direction of the calling voice.

"GET BACK TO YOUR OWNER, THIS MINUTE! NOW!"

To my amazement and relief they did just that. They left Jesse alone and slunk away.

I found it quite intolerable that dogs should see Jesse as a weak victim, even whilst I understood that they are only following their instinct. It was truly heartbreaking.

I also realised for the first time, that although I had known for a long time that Jesse would defend me with his last breath, same was true the other way round. Both of these situations brought out completely instinctive reactions in me. I did not stop to think about wisdom or safety, I just had only one thought which was to take care of Jesse and defend him at whatever cost to myself. I realised what a long way I had come from the diffident anxious person who had first met Jesse. Now I was strong enough to take on all comers, regardless of my safety, at least, I was for Jesse's sake. I had always been intimidated by Alsatians, Rottweilers and Dobermans, but I hadn't even hesitated to face them down. It seems I had indeed become a very different person now from the person whom Jesse had first encountered.

These encounters with dogs who were trying to attack Jesse reminded me of a famous quote by the Chinese philosopher Lao Tzu, founder of Taoism, who lived in the 7th century BC, and whose sayings contained so much wisdom, and in this fast changing world, hold as much truth as ever:

"Being deeply loved by someone gives you strength, while loving someone deeply gives you courage".

How very true this is of the effects of the deep and constant love which flowed between Jesse and me.

How it all ended

Christmas is a very busy time for a church organist, especially when there are choirs involved, and I was worried about how Jesse would cope with the increased activity. He was amazing and still accompanied me to most of the practices and venues at which I was singing, or playing. If I thought a particular occasion would be too stressful for him, my friend would kindly come and stay with him in the house, to keep him company and monitor his health, as I felt continually on edge that he might suddenly have some sort of health crisis. This worked very well, and enabled us to have a last Christmas together, whilst I could discharge my responsibilities to the various musical organisations in which I was involved.

However, in January 2017, 2 years and 3 months after his diagnoses, he began to show signs of pain and unhappiness. The weakness in his left front leg returned, and he began to stumble. He could no longer sit on a carpet, as his front legs just slid from under him, and he ended up lying down. He developed an awkward gait, as he struggled to make his legs work. He started looking longingly at other dogs playing, but made no attempt to try to join them, as he knew he couldn't. We both became depressed, as the walks got shorter and the amount of time spent in the house with him lying around or dozing became longer. He became very dependent and was frantic if he thought I was going to leave him, even to go to the shop for a few minutes, and our lives virtually ground to a halt.

His kidneys were not doing too well, as he needed to go out every hour and a half, day and night, which meant I got little sleep, which made life more difficult to cope with.

I took him to the vet and asked for more pain relief, and it did reduce the levels of pain (I could read this in his eyes) but made him a bit more sleepy and slow on walks. Even so, he never trailed behind me, but determinedly trotted ahead, albeit stopping regularly to make sure I was still there. At home, he still came upstairs with me, although it was a bit of a struggle.

The end came quite suddenly when he developed 'foot drop'. This occurs when the leg is too weak to lift the paw properly and it drags on the ground, causing pain and bleeding as well as dysfunction. It is normally seen in the hind legs, where it is more manageable, but in Jesse it was that front leg which had given him trouble before. I spent two weeks trying to find him a protective boot, but none of them fitted, and none of my creative attempts to make a substitute worked. A friend of mine who had an industrial sewing machine even made him a boot, but it got scraped through, by Jesse dragging his paw on the pavement, in no time at all. As well as dragging the paw, which made it bleed, Jesse stumbled frequently, as his other 3 legs were weak by now, and unable to cope with the loss of function in his front paw.

I had bought him a ramp to help him get into the car several weeks previously, but now he struggled with that, as his front legs weren't strong enough to cope. We managed, by me half lifting him, and his hind legs helping, but it was not easy. We went to grassy areas, where he would not damage his foot so much as it dragged along the ground, but he could only manage 10-15 minutes before he was too tired to carry on.

One day we were on a hill, a walk near home, which he had always enjoyed. He tripped and stumbled and couldn't right himself. He rolled over and over until he got to the bottom of the hill and landed, winded, in a heap. I massaged his limbs, and talked to him soothingly, telling him he would be OK soon, and by some miracle, nothing was broken and he eventually got up and we were able to get home.

But I realised, deep inside, that we had reached the end, and I had to find the courage to take him to the vet, so he could die peacefully before he had some awful traumatic accident, like breaking a bone, falling as he crossed the road and being run over, or just waking up in the morning unable to move, as his right front leg was now very weak as well. His breathing was laboured, and it was obvious the cancer was also closing in on him.

Some people try to keep their dogs alive as long as possible, as they can't bear to part with them, or they feel they should let nature take its course, and of course, everyone has a right to their own opinions and their own sense of what is best for their dog, but I felt that Jesse's quality of life was the most important factor. He had always been such an active dog, so full of life and enthusiasm, and had also been a dignified dog, and to see him struggling and stumbling and falling over was more than either of us could bear. I could tell that he was trying so hard to cope, and feeling pretty awful most of the time, and that we had both reached the point where we couldn't fight any longer. The end was very near, and we had been unable to overcome his illnesses. We had done everything we could , but it seemed as inevitable as the tide coming in, that his life was about to come to an end, and I wanted to be ahead of the game, so that it ended as gently and peacefully as possible, once we were quite sure that there was no chance at all of recovery.

The following morning I phoned the vet and explained our situation. He arranged to see us that evening to discuss it. We spent that last day as normally as possible, although I spent a lot of time stroking him and just being around him. We went for a last very short walk, and on the way back he was struggling so much that I would have carried him if he had been a smaller dog. He looked up at me, and I think he realised he just couldn't go on any more, despite our best efforts, and we had to let each other go. When we saw the vet, he just took one look at Jesse, noted his rapid deterioration, and agreed we had hit a brick wall. I wanted Jesse to think it was just a routine visit, and he went on the scales as he always did, and offered his paw for the injection, as he always had for his blood tests. There was no panic, no fear, just a routine visit to the vet's, he would have thought. Or maybe he didn't. Maybe he knew this was the end, as he usually put up some resistance to the blood tests, but this time he just lay completely still. I expect he was so tired, from trying to go on against increasingly heavy odds that even he had finally given up. I held it all together and just encouraged and comforted him, no tears, or fuss, nothing which would have frightened or upset him, until after he quickly and peacefully died. Then, as the tears flowed I told him again that I would love him always and forever, and he would always be with me in my heart. I asked God to bless him and watch over him, and left.

Everyone at the vet's was very kind and sympathetic, and I went straight to my friends' house and was looked after by them. Close family and friends have been supportive and understanding ever since he died, and have helped me along this awful lonely road.

I don't know how you learn to live without someone who was so very special, and with whom you had shared so much love, but I do know we managed to have a couple of extra years together, standing shoulder to shoulder, fighting these evil diseases every inch of the way, and we went on until the very last ditch. I also know that they were good years, with lots of fun and happiness and that until the last two or three weeks, Jesse had a good quality of life, which he appreciated and enjoyed to the full. No-one could say it was an easy two years, but we did it, together, and it was worth every worry, every sleepless night and every tear. Every second together was precious, and I'm quite sure we both felt the same about that.

After his death, many kind people commiserated with me, and the most commonly uttered phrase was: "They are like part of the family, aren't they?" I would nod and try to smile, knowing they were meaning to be kind, but actually they were way off the mark, because the truthful answer is:

"NO, he was NOT like part of the family. He was part of ME, and that's a very different thing".

When someone you love so much dies, you go on loving them, even though they are not there. It is a strange feeling, because there is nothing for that love to feed on, except memories, and photos, and a very sad feeling, as the love brings with it an overwhelming sense of loss and missed opportunities, and thoughts about all the extra happy times you could have had, but never did, and never will, as he is not there to enable them to happen.

The photos I had of Jesse only served to underline the fact that he was no longer here with me, and to remind me of the immeasurable happiness I had lost when he died. The memories were so painful sometimes that I had to try to shut them out, and think of other things.

However, people tell me that although it may be that loss is the overwhelming feeling at first, as time goes by, photos really will trigger happy memories, as they are supposed to, and one day, maybe I will be able to smile over them and my many memories, and re-live some of the wonderful times we had together with happiness, rather than sorrow in my heart.

The future is a void, and it is hard not to think of what might have been. I have no idea how I am going to manage without him; I simply can't imagine how I will. However, the body may die, the soul may depart, but the love, I know, will go on forever.

I was indeed fortunate to have such a wonderful dog, and in time I pray that the memory of the good times will predominate. He will always live on in my heart, and I will love him always and forever.

Epilogue: 20.05.2019

Tomorrow is the anniversary of Jesse's birth. He would have been 14, not a bad age for a Border Collie, but by no means old. It is two years and four months since he died. I think of him a great deal, every day, and every night. In all truth I cannot say I miss him any less than I did when he first died.

At first, after his death, I felt totally numb, and unable to do anything at all. I wandered around in shock, not really able to believe that he had gone forever. Then I started going for walks without him, the same walks we had done together, as if he was still there. That was really awful. My son gave me two weeks' free membership of the gym he attended, in the hope of giving me another interest, but I hated it, and just wanted to be outside in the countryside, with Jesse once again. I couldn't play and I couldn't sing because it brought back too many memories of Jesse being there, and I couldn't do it without him. I felt as if someone had put me in a box and shut the lid, and there was no way out. I couldn't bear to do anything without him, yet because he wasn't there I couldn't do anything with him, which left me with nowhere to go.

Thanks to an excellent counsellor who was both sympathetic and very skilled, I overcame this feeling and slowly began to realise that it was not disloyal to Jesse to carry on a life without him, and in fact that he would have hated to see me so upset and dysfunctional. He had always hated it when I was unhappy, and had done everything he could to make things better for me. In fact the best memorial I could give him was to pick myself up and go on with my life, even though he was no longer there to share it. Everything seemed so empty and meaningless without him, and it was really hard to motivate myself. I also experienced something which I understand is common in bereavement. I would see a black and white collie in the distance and think it was Jesse, and then realise it couldn't be, and it was like losing him all over again. This happened repeatedly over a long period of time. However, I had in the back of my mind that Jesse loved life so much, and was so very reluctant to die, that he would have been very cross with me for wasting the life I still had, which he would have given so much to have continued to share.

The lack of confidence and anxiety which had followed me all my life came back, and I lost loads of weight because I didn't really think about eating any more. But gradually, thanks to the support of people close to me, and the healing power of time, I began to improve. I realised that everything Jesse had given me, the courage, and confidence, the self belief, the ability to live in the moment and enjoy life to full could still stay with me, even though he himself had had to leave me. I also came to understand that although he couldn't be with me physically any more, he could in fact remain with me in spirit and always be a part of me in my heart. As I gathered strength and regained some of the courage he had given me, I began to pick up the threads of my life once more, and then I realised that somehow his spirit, his soul, his essence, call it what you will, had never left me and would always be integrated into mine; he really had become part of me forever in a way that is hard to explain. It does not mean that I don't believe his spirit is free to go where it will, or that he is imprisoned within me, but just that he is there, he has somehow left me with a little bit of himself that encapsulates completely who he was and is, and is now so firmly entrenched within me that complete separation is not a possibility. Do I derive some comfort from this? Yes, I do.

I would give everything I possess to have him back here with me, physically, but since that's not going to happen this is, I guess, as good as it gets. Jesse has become a part of what is best in me, and he will never leave, of that I feel sure. He has left me a better person than he found, both physically and mentally. Incorporated deep within me now, is some of his courage, faithfulness, loyalty, willingness to forgive, sense of fun , ability to live in the moment and even, on the good days, a little of his joie de vivre. And yes, sometimes I can now look at photos and smile!

Printed in Great Britain
by Amazon

42071910R00112

Printed in Great Britain
by Amazon

42071910R00112